To Nelson

Happy 88th birthday

Before The Pen Runs Dry...

by

BILLY DILWORTH

Billy Dilworth

March 27, 1997

Published by
Rainmaker and Associates, Inc.

ISBN 0-9655242-0-5

Library of Congress Catalog Card Number 96-070887
Copyright 1996

Printed by
LifeSprings Resources
Franklin Springs, Georgia

Acknowledgments

- To Mom and Dad, who loved, and cared and endured.

- To Joyce, a complete support system; and a real soul-mate.

- To cousins too numerous to mention, but who were more like brothers and sisters, and whose names are sprinkled throughout this volume.

- To Dr. Max Kent, who went the extra mile.

- To Dr. Kenneth Smith, who went the same distance.

- To Dr. John B. Martin, who literally kept us alive.

- To Dr. Christie Winkler, who put us back together after a near-fatal auto crash in Commerce.

- To Dr. and Mrs. Sam Vickery of Commerce and Dr. and Mrs. Billy Ford of Lavonia, all of whom know what medical house calls and true family practice are all about.

- To the late Dr. Roy O. McClain and family, who had faith in a country boy, at times too shaken to pray in a big church, but the preacher knew we needed prayer.

- To Jack and Mary Gillespie, who stand like family through thick and thin.

- To Wilbur Fitzgerald, whom you know as "D. A. Darnell" on television's "In the Heat of the Night," and his wife, Dianna.

- To Greg Pitts of the *Franklin County Citizen*; Linton Johnson of the *Elbert County Examiner*; and Jere Ayers of the *Comer News* and the *Danielsville Monitor*, for keeping the faith.

- To Bobbie Foster of WCON Radio, Gene and Irene Bollinger of WLET Radio, Allen Power of WESC Radio and Matt and Jeanette Phillips of WRIX-FM Radio for continuing support.

- To a bunch of good secretaries, all of whom had the patience of Job, and to Gaynelle Thomason, who holds the distinction of working for one company for 36 years, but has covered just about that many miles in this venture in two years.

- To Elaine Brady, whose computer wizardry is appreciated, and Curt Anderson, for an outstanding cover design.

- And finally, to Sammy Smith, who showed bravery as editor and publisher of this first book.

Foreword

Before The Pen Runs Dry... the title came to us out of the blue in the middle of the night in some faraway space years ago, and kept tugging there. Here it is, the topic of our first book in 1996.

Books have become a dime a dozen in the past two decades, but there is nothing wrong with reading, remembering and stirring the mind; and hopefully, stirring and remembering will be the key points in this volume.

A thin, gangly, frail young boy from Red Hill, Ga. grew up in the cotton patch and enjoyed every moment of picking the white, fleecy cotton from ripe bolls in an era when no one thought about air conditioning, but there was a growing feeling, back in Red Hill in Franklin County in the 1950s, that cotton would soon see its day. Even then, we bought every newspaper within grasp, and the same is true today.

A lot has happened since the 1950s and completion of our journalism studies at the University of Georgia in Athens. Then, more than today, we have been wonderfully blessed with many joyous experiences in the Fourth Estate.

Column-writing, again in 1951, when James Little of the *Lavonia Times* offered space for us to do the Red Hill News — an assignment that was to last through four years of college — and columns initially written by Dad and Mom.

But dads and moms can only do so much; and finally we were told we had asked for the job, and the job was ours.

For years, we poked through the valleys and shadows of Red Hill, and ferreted out story ideas that ultimately would fill whole pages of *The Times*, now the *Franklin County Citizen*.

Columns continued on a daily basis for the Anderson, S.C. *Independent*, the *Atlanta Times*, the *Athens Daily*

News, the *Hartwell Sun,* and ultimately for numerous weekly newspapers across northeast Georgia and western South Carolina.

This, then, is the culmination of four decades of our columns, and the fact remains that writing for the Lavonia paper only yielded a borrowed typewriter, later returned, free postage, and lined paper for handwritten columns before the use of the typewriter. That means seven years of writing for zero dollars and cents, but it was handsome pay for a youngster who needed to grow up quickly.

Many names are mentioned in this book, and there will be topics covering virtually every subject known since the early 1950s.

And that just about does it.

We hope you will enjoy reading *Before The Pen Runs Dry,* because the ink has flowed all too freely, lo, these many years.

An open letter to the new babe, 1996

Dear 1996:

This is an annual letter to you and your counterparts and has been for 26 years.

You will soon be a week old, and you may be whimpering a bit, but the main thing is, you're ours. Perhaps you want to know a little about the old gentleman, 1995. He was a burden for many and a savior for a few.

President Bill Clinton finished his third year, with the approval rate increasing to 60 percent, largely because of his support for the elderly and the sick, and his defense of the Medicare and Medicaid programs, portions of which a man like Newt Gingrich would like to destroy, but he failed miserably in the realm of health care, which may pave the way for insurance companies, doctors and prescription costs to go even higher in your year.

The year, 1995, evaporated into the shadows, with many of us still wondering whatever happened to true friends.

Oh, there are still those fair-weather friends who are with you when the weather is fine. They swim in your pool in July and drink your punch or liquor, and forget about the favors in December. That sort of gratitude isn't worth much.

And 1995 had its Bosnia, and we still do. Lord knows, we hope the President is right, and if he is, that peace on earth and good will on earth will exist in that part of the globe.

Young lad, you will see a lot of unusual happenings in 1996, if you are anything like the fellow before you. There will be more airplane crashes, and 1995 had enough of its quota. There will be the car wrecks, murders, and the gamut. You will probably tire of seeing people on television hold up their hands and say, "Stop the violence," and then the following morning newscasts will show another series of murders as we head for the Olympics.

Really, it doesn't make a lot of sense that so much ado is being made about the Olympics when the whole cotton picking thing will only last for 14 days.

Unluckily for you, 1996 will be a year for elections from city halls to the White House, and there will be so much mud-slinging, every major building in every Georgia city, small and large, will be covered with muck and mire.

Young lad, you will still find a generation of people with a mania for money and sports, and both can be mentioned in the same breath. Hardly a day goes by without a professional sport siphoning multi-millions of dollars, and baseball took a backseat because of the foolishness of million dollar players, and the exhibition of money power on the part of owners, but at least some people saw the world still turns without a major league ball hitting a glove.

There is another mania that will bother you. One football player can draw thousands of dollars per touchdown, while a poor old couple who worked their fingers to the bones, and who worked hard all their lives, will draw a scant $450 a month in Social Security. The system isn't right.

You will have several loudmouths to contend with in 1996. Three who come to mind at the moment include Newt Gingrich, who may be speaking correctly 90 percent of the time, but become a loose cannon the other 10 percent.

The second is Jesse Helms of North Carolina, who will do all he can to protect tobacco interests, when smoking is killing a lot of people. Not so much as heart attacks and AIDS, but who's to say tobacco may not weaken immune systems to allow these diseases to take over like a brush fire?

A third man who may spell trouble is Sen. Phil Gramm of Texas, who claims he was born in Columbus, Ga. and finished school at the University of Georgia, but he doesn't think for one minute like the late Dean of Men, William Tate, who had more common sense in one finger than Gramm's whole body.

One ray of hope for the Republicans is Sen. Bob Dole, who can sometimes leave a bad impression, but at least seems sincere, and did lose an arm in combat defending his country.

Today, ours is a nation with 1,001 religions, and precious little real religion. Tiny churches, sometimes no bigger than a phone booth, seem to be sprouting up on every corner, but the world doesn't seem to be getting any better.

There are millions of folk with computer-like minds, who think they have all the answers without bothering to hear the questions, and there are still fanatics walking around in the name of religion, and many are on television on Sunday mornings, holding a Bible as a prop in their right hand, and begging for money with their left hand, and who knows what's happening to the money.

The positive point to make, young fellow, is there are lots of fine people on the face of the earth that pay their debts, many go to church twice on Sunday and on Wednesday nights. Surprisingly, some good souls never, ever darken the doors of a church, but read their Bibles daily, treat people with brotherly love and turn the other cheek.

You'll like the good folks. Hopefully, this tribe will increase and maybe they will replace the grand scoundrels who deprive and cheat and chisel.

Maybe yours will finally be the year that cancer can be controlled, and perhaps we can forget this talk of curing cancer in your lifetime — a ridiculous statement conceived years ago by the American Cancer Society.

Maybe something can be done about mental depression, and there are at least two drugs out on the market — Prozac and Zoloft, that are performing miracles for many, and pharmacy friends say there are more in the pharmaceutical pipeline that may act more quickly.

Maybe, with God's help, you can assist poor souls with Alzheimer's and AIDS, and a new disease that some say eats away at the skeletal structure.

Would you believe that the year just elapsed saw Americans by the millions turning on silly television talk shows to talk about subjects that should only be discussed in the privacy of the home?

Can you also believe that the pulp magazines are still selling hot items, including all of the tons of some fact and some fiction about O. J. Simpson in Los Angeles?

Well, we'll close for now, and that's enough for a young lad like you to digest anyway.

Gee, you'll be red-faced because of your newness, but take heart, knowing you have a brand-new slate and a whole year out there.

Step carefully, young friend, and Godspeed.

Sincerely,
Billy Dilworth

Learning life through death

Six strong men carried a coffin a good 200 yards — from the side of a mountain road to the top of a mountain here minutes before noon Thursday.

For a moment — a brief second — the whole world seemed to stop as Lloyd Hunter, the funeral director, put his right hand in motion for the driver of a big truck spewing rocks to stop while the pallbearers carried the coffin up the steep hillside to a family cemetery.

The driver complied, and the crowd looked up anxiously and wondered silently if indeed the six could make the trek. They did.

In a way, the whole scene looked so much like the motion picture, "I'd Climb the Highest Mountain," and the funeral and burial in that picture.

This was no simulated scene Thursday, however. It was real life, real tears and real sorrow.

The widow, dressed in black, holding the hands of two sons, wearing number 83 and 84 football jerseys, and the pre-teenaged daughter looked stunned.

This was a raw fact of death.

We wondered how many people in this town failed to pause even for a second — like the truck driver who waited.

And we wondered how many people in this mountain village the man in the coffin had befriended in his life.

A good crowd was present for the services. In fact, the village church was virtually filled — a testimony to the fact the area loved him.

But there was the still hanging question of how many more folk could have closed their doors of business for an hour in memory of a good man.

It's true in every American hamlet — ranging from the city of a million to the community of less than 100.

People don't stop much anymore. Even in death.

The hectic pace goes on, the store stays open, the cash registers still click — even as the final words are spoken for the folk who go on to their reward.

Surely, American people know better. Certainly, human beings can stop to bury the dead.

No doubt about it. This mania for too much in the country must stop or mankind will drown in its selfish juices.

Often, it's strange how we learn life through death.

First job paid the sum of $40 per week

Often, it is difficult to return. Mankind expects to find things as they were, and they aren't, and that hurts.

It was that way here Monday. Anderson is where we spent more than a decade as a young, energetic, green reporter eager to cover the news and reach wreck scenes before other members of the media.

Anderson is where we learned about the boarding house reach first-hand at Mrs. Nellie Mullenix's place on North McDuffie Street.

Anderson is where we found out about life and visiting friends on North Fant Street.

Anderson is where we worked until midnight and 1 a.m. There were no early deadlines and events happening until 11 p.m. got in the paper and food time arrived anywhere from 2 to 4 a.m.

Sometimes, there was breakfast of ham and eggs and toast at the Pure Oil Truck Stop on U.S. 29 toward Hartwell. It was a time to tune in Nashville, Tenn., and hear Ralph Emery on his all-night show or put a quarter in the juke box at the truck stop to get six plays of Don Gibson or Kitty Wells and the other pure-country crowd.

Anderson is where we learned about life at the John C. Calhoun Hotel after the boarding house days. It is where we saw an evangelist pretending to be blind earlier in the night sitting on his bed and counting out $50 as a single offering and laughing gleefully at how he "fooled the crowd."

Anderson is where we met newspaper friends like Slim Hembree and Jim Blessing and Hank Acker and Jim Brown and Frank Lee and Frank Dickson and the good Lord knows how many more.

Anderson is where we found out firsthand about the Anderson Fair staged every year by I.V. Hulme.

It is where we first went to work for Wilton E. Hall at the paper for the sum of $40 per week as a student intern in 1953.

Anderson is where we rode our first escalator at Bailes Department Store downtown.

It is where we dropped in at Dixon-Powers Drug Store on Main Street for an afternoon bite of ice cream in a cup topped with nuts.

Anderson is where we talked with dozens of people each night on the telephone and always asked them to "come to see us at the office some time."

We don't get back much anymore.

Most of the time, it is to doctors' offices, the hospital, and to funerals.

A trip about town Monday was revealing in a number of ways:

The boarding house is gone and green grass, along with a few wild onions, is there now.

The places on North Fant have changed occupants no telling how many times.

The truck stop on U.S. 29 closed a long time ago, and only the building still stands.

The Calhoun Hotel is still a structure, but it's mostly an apartment building now and the young "evangelist" may be fleecing the public in bigger cities these days.

The Anderson Fair is going full blast each fall. I.V. Hulme died several years ago.

Slim Hambree and Frank Dixon are dead, Jim Brown is deceased. Jim Blessing and Hank Acker left this earth a few years ago for better journalism up there in heaven.

Wilton E. Hall, the paper's publisher, died years ago and his widow lives in the family home on the Boulevard.

The drug store has changed ownership a number of times and Lord only knows what happened to all the people who took the first precriptions of tranquilizers called Equanil and Librium.

Bailes Department Store closed years ago, and no one seems to know what happened to the town's first and last escalator.

Time has taken its toll on Anderson as it does any place.

But going back and expecting to find a little of the past, and not succeeding, is a trauma.

Except, this time, it's called growing old.

Dear Santa: please bring peace to Earth, humanity

A perfect Christmas, 1990, would see:

• Three inches of snow on the ground and yards of smiles from kids and adults on the inside.

• Going back to Grandma's house and sitting around a long table capable of accommodating 30 people and hearing Aunt Carlene and her daughters asking guests if they wanted iced tea or coffee. The tables were groaning beneath the weight of the food and homemade cakes and pies.

• A country at peace.

• A world at peace.

• A state at peace without bickering between the Speaker of the House and Gov. Elect Zell Miller.

• Peace in the family and a shucking off of all the little jealous details putting brother against brother, sister against sister, cousin against cousin and most of it sadly involves real estate. Which is really not ours after all.

• Hearing good Christmas sermons from Dr. Henry Fields, pastor of Toccoa First Baptist Church, the Rev. T. M. Oliver, a good soul who has preached for years in the Pentecostal Holiness Church, the Rev. Doug Brown of Carnesville—Allens—Fairview—Methodist Churches, the Rev. Richard Bielski of Lavonia First Baptist, the Rev. Doug Ferguson, who just arrived on the scene at Pleasant Hill Baptist Church at Lavonia, and that grand old soul with the the silver hair, the Rev. Roy W. Melton, who has preached in Athens, Elberton, Royston, Hartwell, Lavonia, Martin, Toccoa, and several churches in South Carolina and is still going strong.

• A child's eyes beaming while watching the lighting of the tree, the opening of gifts and the first sight of a toy that caught his or her fancy months ago on a department store shelf.

• The love of a wife, the brown-eyed blond who says, "I love you a lot," and means it.

• A good solid meal of the basics of chicken and turkey, home-made dressing, appropriate vegetables, and a banana pudding.

• A chocolate cake from Talmadge Carter's of Lavonia. He's never tired of that cake.

• The excited voices of family members mingling and hugging and holding and, hopefully, praying before enjoying the holiday dinner.

• Clean sheets and soft pillows on a bed after 364 days of labor.

• Seeing good clean shows on television, not the shoot'em-up type or the gushy Hollywood productions keeping video stores going on practically every other street corner in a major town.

• The sound of silence at a condo in the mountains at Dillard and, suddenly, the whole world seems at peace.

• People who remember the less fortunate, the youngsters who would smile over a 75-cent item, and concern for an old person with nobody to lean on in a rest home.

• More of us taking the attitude of giving rather than receiving. Merry Christmas, everyone!

Young reporter covered UGA integration

People and landscapes change so quickly. The year was 1961, the scene was the University of Georgia, and two blacks, Hamilton Holmes and Charlayne Hunter, were on the threshold of making history. The two walked under the historic arch in downtown Athens, and became the first to integrate the previously all-white school.

A flock of eager beaver reporters was there.

And then it all flashed back in the mind.

Hamilton Holmes, head of orthopedics at Grady Hospital in Atlanta, had died in his sleep from what his physicians said was going to be a complete recovery from open heart surgery.

Channel 2 in Atlanta opened the newscast with a film clip of the 1961 story and there, walking alongside Dr. Holmes and Mrs. Hunter was a thin, pale reporter from Anderson, S.C. named Dilworth.

The memory bank worked overtime.

Back then, we looked on Hamilton Holmes as a young man, and I thought we were far older, but age does that to youth and then to the old.

Dr. Holmes was just seven years our junior, and it was actually youth covering youth.

What a historic moment, and then we thought how fortunate and blessed we were to cover the story, and to have the film for posterity, and to still be alive and breathing God's good air, and maybe it's the reporter in us that still wonders what's around the corner.

A look back at Red Hill, Ga.

One sure sign of a man beginning to reach the elderly side of life, they say, is taking stock of yesterday—or, simply said, looking backward.

Well, it may be so, and if that's the case, we are guilty.

Anyway, the other day we got to thinking of some Sunday afternoon football, baseball, and basketball games played in front yards and cow pastures over in Red Hill, Ga.

We thought at the time—and still believe—that some of the nation's best sports material could be right there in the Franklin County farming area.

No, don't laugh.

Red Hill, a thriving sector recognized on all the Rand-McNally maps put out by oil companies, has provided many a good quarter-back, pitcher, and basketeer.

Trouble is, there were no scouts around to make the discoveries.

The community was unique in that it had two or three dozen young boys who didn't spend their Sunday afternoons making drags in automobiles. Probably this was true because nobody's father was wealthy enough to buy a car for youngsters to tear up—and perhaps this saved a few lives.

While many other areas had young folks playing drop the handkerchief, or ring around the rosies, our group was playing rock-'em, sock-'em football.

Oh, there were the disagreements—the times when some threatened to quit playing.

But, these moments passed—and the games lasted until the Mamas called for the milking and hog slopping chores to be done.

Red Hill, Ga., may never produce a nationally-known athlete, but it will be because nobody was looking at the right time.

Yes, there was Elvis on the train

Paying respects may be one thing some of the human race doesn't have a good track record of anymore, and that thought rang through in our mind as we rushed to Greenville to Thomas McAfee Funeral Home near the middle of this bustling city the other day.

We drove to say goodbye to George Leeman, 61, who married a first cousin, Frances Davis, daughter of Uncle Lonnie and Aunt Effie Davis. Perhaps the reason the conscience was tugging was that George Leeman showed a country boy from Red Hill how to board a train in Greenville in 1957.

Our parents had taken the thin, frail, lanky kid, who had only been accustomed to the cotton patch and a little greener pastures at the University of Georgia, prior to joining the staff of the *Anderson Independent*, and one of our first duties was the once-in-a-lifetime assignment to accompany the South Carolina FFA delegation to Kansas City, Mo., where youthful farm kids from all over the United States gathered for the national convocation.

George and Frances had not been long married when we talked about the upcoming trip, and although he was only one year older, showed the Red Hill boy how to board the Southern passenger train, and how to find the sleeping bunk. That was tremendous indeed, and a great transition, when the closest we had ever been to a train was putting pennies on the track at Olin Pierce's place in Avalon, when the train rolled from Toccoa to Lavonia.

George was like a brother that night, and seemed to assure that everything would be all right and the trip would be good.

The man did not know how correct he was.

Because it was on that journey we met Elvis Presley at Memphis, Tenn., where the rock and roll idol was to board to go to God knows where.

Somehow, the sensitive ears of the reporter got the news and we got off the train at Memphis, and despite would-be intervention from four burly bodyguards, we managed to get a 15-minute interview with Elvis.

"I want to talk to this young man," said Elvis, and the bodyguards backed away. We talked about his music and his upbringing, and our common denominator of coming from single-child families.

The FFA'ers in our delegation could not believe their ears and eyes when they saw the interview taking place, and we called the story in to the paper, and the late Jim Blessing and the late Slim Hembree properly played it above the fold on page one.

Two days later, we were in the Truman Library at Independence, Mo., scarcely a stone's throw from Kansas City, a fact we did not learn until then.

And the former President took time to walk into his office, occupied a chair and hosted the entire South Carolina bunch, including the timid reporter with the bow-tie.

We will never forget a comment he made about dogs and trees, and the only people who know "Give 'em Hell Harry" would know what he meant. But he had an audience of country boys who knew.

That meeting also made the front page of the Anderson paper.

Then, as we walked into the funeral home chapel, these two events unfolded again and seemed as fresh as the morning paper. We may not have made the trip had it not been for the encouragement of good parents and George Leeman and Wilton Hall, who published the Anderson paper for years.

Thankfully, we passed along our thoughts to Mr. Leeman in a letter dated May 17, 1995, when he was spending his last days suffering from cancer of the lung.

The last years had not been easy for the man, who underwent two surgical procedures, but had the support of his wife, Frances, five sons and one daughter.

Mr. Leeman was thin all his life because he never minded work and spent many years as an auto mechanic.

Another Georgia first cousin, Jimmy Carter in Lavonia, who stayed for the funeral, said the preacher talked about George Leeman's acceptance of Christ and of his knowledge that he was going to a better place.

Back in 1957, George Leeman consoled the country kid in the middle of that train, and the other day, a Baptist preacher consoled his family in a funeral home chapel, where many Davis funerals have been held since the early 1950's.

A man—a message

Little more than a decade ago, a man, in his 30s, left the Palmetto State for work in Atlanta—a city even then on the verge of the million-population mark.

He began working with the multitudes with new ideas, and talking of things rarely discussed anymore in a so-called modern age—of sin and wrongdoing.

He was the pastor of a big downtown Atlanta church — one that some of its more concerned members feared was headed, like the general merchandise store, into oblivion.

But — that was not to be.

Under his leadership, the church — First Baptist — has become the South's largest.

And its strength is more than in mere numbers. Some of the finest residents of the entire world hold membership there, and attend services every time its doors are opened.

They have a Leader — with a Message.

This past week, the native South Carolinian drove from Atlanta, through Athens, where he admired the growing, pretty University of Georgia campus, before going on to Anderson — for a week-long series of revival services in Anderson's First Baptist Church.

His messages here have left Anderson area folk stunned. Never before have they heard such powerful preaching.

His voice is not preacheristic. His words, more than just a sermon, are a lesson for life.

This man is not afraid. He preaches to all — to Mr. Big with three degrees — and to the man only able to mark an "X" where a signature ought to be.

He talks plainly — of an old, old — yet so freshly-new story.

He preaches three more times today — at 9 and 11 a.m. and 7:30 p.m.

His name? Dr. Roy O. McClain, who once said the railway from Donalds to Due West wasn't as long as others, but the tracks were just as wide.

What a refreshing attitude in an age that needs sound and sober thinking so much!

More memories flow at funeral in Lavonia

Going back the second time in a month to a funeral in Franklin County marked another rekindling of old memories and oh, how they linger.

This time, it was the funeral for Mrs. Alice Clinkscales Williams, 73, devoted wife to the late Dr. J. W. Williams, Jr., and a mother to two sons and two daughters.

Somehow, Mrs. Williams never seemed to grow weary, and that was unusual because the life of a country doctor and a country doctor's family is never simple, and probably was never planned to be. Her husband remarked on many occasions that he was probably the last of the medical breed to make house calls — and that was essentially correct, especially on a wholesale basis — because Dr. Williams went, regardless of weather, financial conditions or an illness that was to be terminal in a short time anyway.

Like the four preachers said, Mrs. Williams had a tremendous mind, taught school and Shakespeare, but her unending thoughts were on her family and her God.

Each Christmas, she penned a poem, which she wrote in longhand, and distributed copies to numerous people in all corners of the world. That was her way of witnessing, and who is to say that such a great literary talent did not outdo what multi-millions of us don't do and could?

Going back this time meant travel to Weldon Funeral Home, and a big color portrait of the late Freddie Weldon had the reservoir of memories going. Mrs. Weldon was there, son Chip, and three capable employees named Howard and David Whitworth, and Mrs. Weldon's brother, Byron Toney.

Serving as a pallbearer again was also reminiscent of the old days, and especially as the procession made a special trip around the lovely Williams home before going on to the church and hearing the good preachers, church hymns by the organist, and a beautiful vocal solo by Ricky Whitworth.

But especially reminiscent was the ride Larry Cabe took with us in our car, while Andy Hill, prominent Lavonia attorney, Wilton Morgan and Tommy Beasley, also of Lavonia, and William Simpson of Iva, S.C., Mrs. Williams' hometown, completed the list of pallbearers.

It was a chance to talk of the old days with Mr. Cabe, and the mind flicked back to reading the *Lavonia Times* in the 1940s telling of his accomplishments as a farm youngster in Red Hill, and we recall how well this young man had done to represent a farm community in this world, and later becoming manager of Georgia Power Company in Lavonia, where he served until retirement.

We talked about his family — his brother, Max Cabe, who died less than two years ago, and of his dear relatives like W. C. Sosby and the other Sosby brothers, Bill Ray, Tom Ed and Jack.

We talked about the passing of time, the contributions of many souls who no longer have earthly worries, and of how often the human mind seems to slip as age progresses.

It was good to see three of Dr. Williams' loyal staff members, Mrs. Doris Rosencrance, Mrs. Janet Brock and Mrs. Elizabeth Crump. No doctor could have had a more loyal, caring staff who proved true, even until the final hour of his funeral.

The memory machine was working overtime when we saw the children and their doctor husbands, and the two sons, all of whom did well, and his only brother, Dr. Lewis Williams of Athens, who later became a member of the powerful State Dental Board.

Although the sun was blazing hot, it did not deter the ability to recall and to think — and maybe all of us ought to do more serious thinking — even if the occasion has to be a funeral.

The 'little house' in Carnesville

The memory bank works overtime when passing the little frame house on the Lavonia highway inside Carnesville's limits. To those over 35, it is the "Dyar house." To the younger set, it is the house which burned and was renovated and painted yellow with gold shutters on the windows. To the people who really love and care, it was "home" for many years for the late Eugene and Ellis Dyar.

Dyar operated *The Carnesville Herald,* and then he died. Mrs. Dyar built the meals, kept the fires going, and continued to make the white house a "home" for years. She lived on memories and a daily dialogue with friends.

She lost a son in World War II and all she kept was his picture, an 8 by 10 on one of the prominent cabinets in the living room.

There was another son, Eugene, Jr., who distinguished himself with a career in the Navy. He advanced so well, they named a ship in his honor and invited his mother to the ceremonies. Someone broke a bottle of champagne at ship side, making it all official.

In later years, after her husband's death, and the son, LaGrande, died for a country that only honored her with a gold star. Mrs. Dyar lived alone in that house.

She drove an old-model Chevrolet and kept it in good running condition. She survived by listening to the radio — to Toccoa by day and on Saturday — to WSM Radio in Nashville by night and on weekends, when there was always the Grand Ole Opry. She met a lot of friends by radio. She was introduced to Ralph Emery, and Mrs. Dyar had the chance to hear him emcee shows in person at Carnesville and Winterville.

She was on a first-name basis, too, with John and Linda Riggs, also from Nashville radio days. She always called them "Mr. Emery" and "Mr. Riggs." One Christmas, in the mid-1970's, John and Linda Riggs knocked on her door in the thick of a winter's evening, and deposited a Christmas present.

Mrs. Dyar visited a lot during the daytime, calling on Mrs. Mack Wansley and Mrs. Edna Phillips, and others in and around town.

One day, she fell and injured her arm and Dr. Max Kent of Anderson, S.C., fixed it. Mrs. Dyar went to near Washington, D.C., to live with her military son and his family. Ray Pritchett took care of her 1949 black Chevrolet car. She never came back to Carnesville alive, but they brought her body back to Royston and buried her alongside her newspaperman husband.

And now Ray Pritchett is dead. He was a good man.

No one knows what happened to the car.

Mrs. Dyar would have shuddered seeing her house blackened by smoke. But she would be happy today knowing it is alive again and its walls are reverberating with human laughter.

They don't make new houses like old houses.

They don't make new people like old people.

And the world is worse because of both.

We're going back to hills

Right soon now, we're going back to the mountains of North Carolina and have another chat with a 98-year-old mid-wife.

It'll be worth driving the 150 miles visiting "Aunt Mattie" Smith, a grand ole soul, who lives in a three-room frame house tucked neatly away in the Smokies.

The 10 miles of narrow, dirt road won't be a bother either.

Talking with "Aunt Mattie" a half hour will enlighten us more than reading a dozen refreshing volumes on keeping good physical and mental health, or hearing a half-dozen discussions on how to make friends and influence people.

You see, the world needs more folks like her.

Last summer, she seemed mightily concerned about the bomb shelter scare, when everybody and his brother felt somebody across the pond might unload with an H-bomb.

"No need for all that haste," the lady said. "Aw, shucks, it's all right if they want to build them, I guess, but I'd hate to know a lot of my flesh and blood and friends was dying, while I sat there hovering for all that dust to settle."

"Aunt Mattie" makes sense on a lot of subjects, we learned.

The present generation?

"They're no worse than teenagers of our times," she said. "Cept parents may be too light in letting their younguns stay out all night courting their fellows."

Television?

"Don't care for it, son," she said, with a certain telling look in her eyes. "May be the devil's workshop. A lot of folks might be working instead of watching that thing."

The end of time?

"Only the Good Lord knows when everything is finished on this old earth," she said. "I reckon someday a lot of these people will quit saying when the world's going to, but will be ready for Him when it does happen."

And what does she say about her duties as mid-wife?

"I helped deliver babies for folks I'd never seen before," she declared. "And I've never seen 'em since. So far as I know, about all the children lived, and I hope they made something out of themselves."

"You see that scrapbook over there in the corner?" "Aunt Mattie" said, pointing to a book, as large as a Sears-Roebuck catalogue, but yellowed with age. "Well, it contains marks of every baby I brought into this world—that is, until I stopped counting at something over 1,400."

Money?

"Aunt Mattie" won't tell you, but her close neighbors say she got nothing but maybe a free meal for delivering the babies in her mountain area.

That's why she doesn't have electric lights and modern conveniences today.

And that's the reason she has to go sparingly on her food.

"Aunt Mattie" isn't the kind of person, though, to want sympathy. She'd talk an hour avoiding the subject.

That's why we're so anxious to go back up in those Carolina hills, and see her again.

Pitiful part about it is that it may be our last time.

"Aunt Mattie" has cancer, but is unaware of it.

She calls it "rheumatiz and authuritis."

And maybe it's best she doesn't know.

A walk down the aisle starts a new life for Billy Dilworth on Sunday at age 56

Seeking a daughter's hand for marriage is something quite common in the 1930s, maybe even 40s, but who's to say it isn't the thing to do in 1990?

With that thought in mind, we walked into the home of Mrs. Mary Shirley at Turnerville, nestled in the hills of Habersham County, and probably seemed a bit more nervous than usual.

Mrs. Shirley stood as she always does and asked us to take a seat.

"Mrs. Shirley," we opened, "we don't have time to sit, but I just wanted to ask you for Joyce's hand."

The gracious little great-grandmother, whose age belies the fact that she's really 85, thought quickly, then answered, "You may not only have Joyce's hand. You may have Joyce."

And, that's the way it went a few months ago.

Getting married at any age is probably a little mind-boggling even for the young, perhaps dipping down into the teen group, but entering the world of matrimony at the then-age of 55 is a little more than mind-boggling.

Oh, you've probably heard the news by now. Joyce Shirley will join us at the Methodist Parsonage in Carnesville this Sunday to exchange "I do" and "I will" in front of three good preachers, the

Rev. Doug Brown, host pastor, the Rev. Jack Gillespie, former pastor and longtime friend and now a Marietta Methodist minister, and Dr. Henry Fields, pastor of Toccoa First Baptist Church. Some people wonder about the three preachers and a few even boldly asked why it took three to marry two in an abbreviated ceremony and that probably deserves an explanation.

Doug Brown is not only our pastor, but also a friend.

Jack Gillespie is not only a former pastor, but also a warm friend who helped preach the final services in the deaths of Dad and Mom.

Dr. Fields has long been aware that we're as much Baptist as Methodist and, in God's eyes, there are really no denominational lines, no state borders, and no county boundaries.

Dr. Fields' mentor was the late Dr. Roy O. McClain, who preached at Atlanta First Baptist Church for more than 17 years, and anybody who's read this column a fortnight knows of the deep respect and love we've had for Dr. McClain, who left us early at the age of 68 a few years ago.

Somewhere, Dr. McClain is looking from above and approving the fact that it will take three ministers to do what one could do.

The decision to hold the ceremony at the parsonage was made mostly because of historical significance. Sixty-four years ago, Dad and Mom exchanged vows in that same spot, and Dad saw himself in a floor-length mirror.

"Preacher, could we turn around? I see my knees shaking," he said. The minister complied.

Joyce is a fine lady, someone we've been knowing better than 20 years.

We had our first date at the Cornelia drive-in theatre back in the so-called era before nuclear weapons, a negative world, and much ado about nothing.

She was in charge of the Hearth Restaurant in Tallulah Falls at the time and we simply asked her out for a cup of coffee. The cup of coffee wound up at the Cornelia drive-in and the main feature was a Bill Anderson country music movie. Little did we realize that the fellow we spent four years of college with at the University of Georgia would be entertaining his old classmate and newfound girlfriend at an outdoor movie less than 40 air miles from Athens and less than 300 miles from Nashville, where Bill filmed the movie.

But all that is history now, and in retrospect, maybe that's the

27

way the good Lord had of introducing us to each other and Joyce to Bill Anderson.

Someone used to say that life begins at 40.

We doubt that.

Life can begin at any age.

How about 56?

Seriously, we hope you'll join the three good preachers by saying a prayer for the two of us as we start a new phase of life.

Thank you for your encouragement, your years of support, your understanding.

And, if anybody should ask you how Dilworth met his new bride, you can tell 'em it all started over a cup of coffee, which probably sold then for a dime.

He doesn't play by 'car'

Monday's On the Road featured a veteran educator named Louie H. Hardy of Carnesville, a gentleman who proudly proclaims education had advanced rapidly since the days of the three Rs.

Toward the bottom of the page one story, reference was made to the professor's hobbies and implied he "plays piano by car."

Well, that would have been a feature story and he would be some professor if he could accomplish that.

Undoubtedly, United Press International would give national play — a school teacher who takes a piano along and plays it in the car.

A reader, Gerald Voyles of Red Hill, called the Lavonia office of *The Daily News* Monday afternoon and wanted to know more about the fellow who plays a piano in the car.

Once the blood pressure settled after initial anger, we explained what happened. Or what did not happen.

Our news copy goes through the telephone line and is fed through a telecopier machine, capable of transmitting entire pages to the main newsroom in Athens.

Blurred copy provided bad reading for the editors in Athens or there was a computer foul-up.

The same thing happened in Sunday's column dealing with the old-timer and his thoughts.

In one paragraph, there was this sentence: "Since our old-time friend was born, our nation was gone through World War I, World War II, Korea, Vietnam and only the Good Lord knows how many mini-conflicts in that time."

Obviously, the word should have been "our nation has gone through..."

Once again, we can relate with the problems encountered by telephone operators who sit at their stations and find their best efforts going awry because of human errors.

Newspapers are far from being exempt.

In fact, since the age of computers, newspapers have seen more errors get by than ever.

True. Our era may be living better and longer in some cases.

But we're not quite to the point of playing a piano in the car.

It's a good thing. The car and the driver couldn't stand it!

Pardon us for a moment, please. "Professor Hardy" is outside the office and word is he is about to play the piano in his car!

Is cart pulling the horse?

The two thoughts sear the mind on this day after human destiny with the Internal Revenue Service.

First, they were talking on radio late Sunday night about the homeless in Atlanta and how the number has grown in the past few years.

A leader in an ongoing project for those people without a top over their heads said the number averages between 7,000 and 8,000 in summer and slightly more in winter.

"The sad fact is," he was saying, "is that fewer than 150 volunteers help us with the homeless and we're in a city with 1,500 active church congregations."

What a commentary!

Less than a dozen hours later, Greg James was on the "Mountain Morning" TV set with us talking about the fact he was depressed because the Atlanta Braves had lost six straight games.

Although making conversation, which is a must in hosting a show, Greg confided off the air that he is a big sports fan.

That's well and good because the mind can't be consumed by work and toil 24 hours a day.

But we said on TV, and repeat in print now, that our era has reached a crazy stage, in which many professional athletes get paid more than $1, $2, and $3-million a year for tossing a baseball, basketball, or football only a few weeks in the year.

Professional sports has largely been taken over by greedy people, who see the sport as a chance to make money in a variety of ways.

And the poor old people out there who pull and support and holler and yell don't realize all of that is not for their benefit, but to pad the pocketbooks of owners and players and others who enjoy slices of the pie.

The positive point to make is that money isn't the bottomline in high school and college sports.

High schoolers and college athletes literally play their britches off in an effort to win and, hopefully, become good sports off the athletic field and floor too.

Could it be we've got the cart pulling the horse and the tail wagging the dog?

After months, we meet the computer

It was inevitable — our meeting the computer.

For months, even years now, this space has seen ink devoted to verbal assaults on the machine that has changed much of mankind and civilization the past two decades.

Some of our comments have been directed at computer operations of the telephone company and a good guy who heads Southern Bell's operations in Gainesville, Athens, Royston, and Elberton, Bert Cloud, tried twice previously to get us to join him in Athens.

The schedule for both agreed to the confrontation of Dilworth and the computer Thursday.

Also present to witness the event were Publisher Bob Chambers and Jack Garner of Macon, district traffic engineer for Bell.

First of all, Southern Bell's operations have changed drastically since the days of an operator answering "central" and the gray-haired lady patching the customers in to another customer up the road at the beauty shop or the service station.

We saw the transition as soon as we entered the big building in Athens — a facility where 12 or 15 ladies were working around a computer-type terminal and answering calls from telephone long-distance customers from much of North Georgia.

Mrs. Anne Youngblood, a patient supervisor for 29 years, joined Cloud in explanation of what was going on, while Chambers and Garner talked about the mechanics.

Actually, the big computer is in Macon, but many inner workings are in Athens and Gainesville, where the calls are distributed evenly.

We met an operator named Janet, a patient individual who answers a half dozen calls, mostly collect, while we watched... The electronic board is capable of flashing in digital figures the number called, or the number calling.

Earlier at lunch, both Cloud and Garner said the volume of calls handled in 1980 could not have been tackled via the old system a dozen years ago.

And we must agree on that point.

Also, there is a basic agreement that it isn't the computer which makes the sometimes-terrible mistakes, but the people, humans if you please, who must feed information into the memory bank.

But, let's be honest.

Our day will have the computer, or the computer's computer, to contend with from now on.

Hopefully, the road ahead looks clear with only a few roadblocks and the people who feed the computer won't err.

Realistically, that may be pipedreaming of the best order.

At any rate, we came away convinced we were more impressed with the computer than it has been of us.

And that may not be all bad either!

'Til the river runs dry

A man with a long beard sat on the front step at Nora's Mill outside Helen the other day and gave a commentary on the country.

"If all the world was like this place, we'd be all right," he said. "Business is good, anybody who wants a job can get one, and we ain't got no real big problems."

"This corn mill has been operating a long, long time and things will be all right here until the Chattahoochee River runs dry," he went on.

What a reflective refreshing glimpse of life from a man approaching 90.

"People have been saying for as long as I remember that the world is going to the dogs," he said. "Well, like a preacher said one time, the dogs have had a mighty long wait."

As the man talked, machinery turned inside the milling operation, where they claim to make the best waterground meal this side of Memphis, Tenn.

A man from Charlotte, N.C., pulled into a parking area, asked the old man who was in charge, and walked inside.

He came out 10 minutes later with two 10-pound sacks of meal in his hands.

"They say this makes good cornbread," the Tar Heel resident declared.

"Make you want to slap your grandpa," the old-timer responded, and the visitor seemed startled.

Maybe he hadn't heard that expression ever.

Life's just a bit different in Helen.

And on this Saturday, it's good to report there's nothing wrong with that!

Saturdays in May are good

Saturdays are good.

Particularly Saturdays in May.

Reasons are abundant.

The weather is mostly nice. And, according to tradition, generally are not too hot.

Nights are good for sleeping, and it is that in-between time when heating and air conditioning are not necessary.

Outside in the daytime, spring is everywhere.

Ladies in their bonnets and men in their straw hats are getting the gardens ready for, hopefully, a bountiful year.

Before long, both the women and men will be bringing in tomatoes and fresh corn and okra.

Saturdays in May are good in other respects.

It's the time to bring on the memory machine and recall when kids weren't too proud to go barefoot and play marbles or go fishing in the creek with little bait and little ammunition otherwise, but with a ton of hope.

Somehow, the hope usually brought back the fish.

May is that time of year which brings the closing of school and the end of sitting in the classroom and hearing about math, English, or the rise and fall of the Roman Empire.

Saturdays in May revive talk of class reunions.

A time for classes of old to band together and talk and eat and marvel at how some students put on weight and lost hair. And just about in that order.

Saturdays in May also bring talk of family reunions and plans for all-day get-togethers.

And this is the time aunts get to kiss all young ones and the young ones start hating family reunions. It turns out to be a vicious cycle.

Saturdays in May are good.

Judge Heard could smell the roses

Too often, mankind tends to proclaim glowing tributes to people after the coffin is sealed and covered with the family wreath.

Not so with Judge Robert Heard of Elberton.

They came by the dozens to the Elbert County Courthouse in Elberton Wednesday to pay honor to an attorney who has devoted a quarter century as State Court Judge and far more than that to helping mankind.

This is good — in more ways than one.

Mainly, and primarily, Judge Heard is fit as a fiddle in a Grand Ole Opry band, or violin in the New York Symphony, and he has good hearing and vision and he knew all that was going on for a couple of hours in the unveiling of his portrait in the upstairs courtroom here.

The tributes were sincere.

"When Judge Heard told you something, you could you put it in the bank," Judge Ray Burrus of Royston said.

"He is a kind, considerate person, he left lawing to lawyers, gave charges of an understanding nature to jurors and boasts an excellent record," Judge William F. Grant, who presided over the ceremonies, reported.

Former Chief Supreme Court Justice H. E. Nichols called him a "man among men."

Attorneys stepped forward and commended the man for multiple-hour days and he appreciated it.

In response, Judge Heard immediately said "hearing all those things is like drinking strong wine. It swells your head."

That's being blatantly honest too.

We think there ought to be more genuine backslapping and medal-pinning and rose-smelling while a man is alive and less after he is gone, but it's too bad the human race doesn't operate that way.

Even in death now, the memory is brief. A so-called friend may check in at the funeral home, sign the register, and the moment is gone.

Judge Robert M. Heard deserved his praise Wednesday and he saw friends driving for miles to make the occasion complete.

"I'm humbled," he told one friend over the years.

That's as good a way as any to sum it all up.

Two lessons in sobering up

A young man, not yet 40, tried to pump gasoline into a brand-new automobile, but the job was tedious because his arms were shaking as he tried to pump and talk.

We didn't mention his plight, obviously, and neither did he, but it had been 20 years since we met.

We grew up together — the two of us. We attended the same school, and it was a chance meeting the other day.

He spent the past eight years in New York City, he said, going from job to job and was totally displeased.

"I had three marriages and none of them worked," he said, his hands shaking as he tried to replace the gasoline cap.

His biggest concern now is his mom, who stays in a nursing home about 25 miles away.

"I check on her three times a week," he said. "Her mind is clear. It's just there's nobody to look after her but me, and I've gotta work."

"And what have you been doing?" he asked.

We tried to fill him in.

Somehow, the two of us caught up on 20 years in about 15 minutes and drove away.

He was shaking badly.

Another five miles down the road and there was another pathetic scene — a man on two crutches walking toward his mobile home but holding on for dear life to a Cocker Spaniel puppy.

He had been to the mailbox — probably looking for a government check.

And there was some serious thinking as we viewed the scene.

We wondered — who is in the better shape — the man with the shaking hands who probably had too much to drink over the years, or the man who had two crutches to help him greet the day?

And then we thought of others much worse — of those who can't walk, can't talk, and who live like vegetables.

A few of those scenes could sober us all up!

Life is like an escalator

Someone said it wisely the other day. Life is like a set of rolling stairs. An escalator, if you please.

When you think about it, this is true.

Some people are always getting on. They're arriving into the world — mostly in hospitals now — a far change from the old days when the majority of people saw the light of day at home.

Others are constantly getting off. It is called death.

Some die easily in hospital beds. Others expire violently in wrecks and wars and varying degrees of statistics.

The writer of a song wrote a tune years ago about "some getting on, some getting off."

And another had a melody entitled, "Stop the world so I can get off."

The world has turned in fast fashion the past few decades and a TV soap opera was tabbed "As The World Turns" in the 1950s. It still carries that title.

Even, with it all, with the ebb tide and flow, human life is much like an escalator.

A bus station, perhaps.

Some are always getting on.

Unfortunately, others are always getting off.

But, at least, there's movement, and that's what counts after all anyway.

The fellow has seen his share

We wrote about him several years ago — the fact he frequently visited the office in Lavonia, dropping by for coffee, and was always one of the sharpest dressers.

A "best-dressed man's list" would have automatically included his name.

His hair was always in place and he smoked the finest mini-cigars.

"Gotta go first class," he said, grinning, and you got the idea he was joking.

He lived for a time in Anderson, S.C., and scored impressively in employment there.

"I'm doing all right, I guess," he would say, "I'd like to be making more money, but I guess that's the same with everybody. We'd always like to be in better shape."

Eight months passed since we last heard from him, and that was when he relayed word by telephone he was taking a new job in South Georgia.

Until one afternoon later when he suddenly dropped into the office again and didn't look like the same guy.

This time, he was wearing overall trousers, a tattered shirt, a hat with the "Ex-Lax" insignia in front and his hair was long — three times longer than the last time we'd seen him.

"Thought I'd stop by and visit," he announced. "I brought one of my friends. He's married with two kids and they're home in another part of the state, while he's in grad school."

We asked how life had been.

"Pretty mixed up," he said. "I didn't stay long with the job after I left Anderson, but I got my debts paid, and now I'm doing nothing."

He could tell the last statement brought surprise.

"How're you getting by?" he was quizzed.

"Barely," he answered.

"No, we're sharing this house out in the country and there's not much rent and I may take a correspondence course and finish college." His voice trailed and he seemed to be thinking.

He knocked on the glass window and motioned to his friend to get out of the car and join him.

"This is ----," he said. "He's a longtime friend." He pointed toward us.

The friend pulled out a can of Prince Albert tobacco and a pack of cigarette leaves and started rolling his own.

"Gotta economize," he said. "These ain't so bad. Before you start thinking this is marijuana, it isn't," said the man who had changed his lifestyle.

"But," he confided, "I've tried it, and that's the one bad thing I have living where I am. You're exposed to it all the time. I don't think I like it that well."

"What's the feeling?" we inquired.

"Oh, in a way, a lot like beer, but it leaves you tired and weak after it's over. It's not my cup of tea," he said.

He leaned over to his married friend and reached for the community Prince Albert can and a pack of leaves. Somehow, he was having a terrible time rolling his own.

Suddenly they got up, both of them said their goodbyes and headed for the car.

"I'll be back to see you," he said. "You may not know me the next time." He showed back up not long ago, and sure enough, his original personality was back. He had just driven off Interstate Highway 85 and had spent the night with a sister in Atlanta after buying two nice new suits.

"I'm back home; I deserted the life I led for a year; and it's good to dress decently again," he continued.

"Maybe it's good to see life's other side. I've seen my share...."

'Tell me about the good old days'

The Judds, a mother-daughter duo, own a hit single making the airwaves these days with a simple title. It's called "Grandpa."

"Grandpa, tell me about the good old days," say the Judds in their song with a pretty melody.

They tell Grandpa that "the world's gone crazy."

And they insist that the old fellow tell them about life when things were simple.

Basically, those people over 40 who grew up on the farm know what they're speaking about.

Why not return to the simple life back on the farm when the father of the household had a pair of mules and followed them all day behind the plow? They were tough, sweaty hours, but they were filled with sincere work and no handouts and sleep came with weariness, not through a medically-prescribed pill.

Why not go back to the days of the church in the wildwood — when they sang old-time hymns like "Rescue The Perishing" and "Almost Persuaded" and "Just As I Am," and not the jazzed-up-songs they call hymns in 1986? Why not a throwback to the era when a man gave a good hour's work for an hour's pay although the pay wasn't much because the people doing the hiring didn't have much?

Why not return to sitting on the front porch and watching the world fly by — instead of flying by in the world and the front porch has changed to condos and the people who build condos don't know the first thing about porches and stirring summer breezes and cooling showers?

Why can't we go back to the times when a man's word was his own bond, and if he told you he'd be at a place at 8 o'clock in the morning, he'd be there at that hour or burst in an effort to keep his schedule?

Why not go back to the days when neighbors visited neighbors and swapped food and vegetables and borrowed flour and sugar and meal, a far cry from today's visit to the convenience store?

Why not go back to the leisurely Sunday afternoons when kinfolk visited and had a good time? Now, the only visiting is done in a halfhearted manner and not much of that is around any more.

Why not dispense with the much ado about nothing in 1986 and the mania for more and the bottom line figure is money, not friendship?

The Judds picked a good song when they chose "Grandpa."

We only wish some of the things they sing about were happening.

But they are all gone with the wind never to return, and that is the sad part of it all.

'It beats dying at home'

By dusk, the former store building is filling with people. They drive to one of four places featuring bingo in this town and there are usually two games operating one night and the other two in full movement other nights.

Only Sunday is devoid of bingo, but they make up for it the rest of the week. They play until dawn the other six days and all day Saturday in Greenville, S.C.

"It beats sitting and dying at home," said one overweight woman who keeps herself fortified with Milky Way candy bars, free hot coffee, soft drinks, and orange slices from K-Mart.

Bingo is a game which brings frowns to the faces of many in Georgia, but produces players galore in many other southern states — South Carolina, Tennessee, and Florida, for example.

In Florida, they play at some church fellowship halls, and the churches benefit from the profits. Which is no worse than money tossed into the collection plates on Sunday morning that may have been earned by other than sweat-of-the-brow efforts, and not a solitary soul says a thing.

Over here, bingo is king.

Some people don't hold down jobs because their employment has been terminated in textile plants in the economic pinch. Instead, they arrive at the bingo houses, sponsored by service and veterans organizations, start early and play late.

They admit chances for winning are greater after midnight when much of the crowd has gone home.

One woman walked out $50 richer Thursday night, but says that is not unusual. A big security-type guard escorted her to the car. They do that for the big winners.

Those who don't win, but lose, don't need an escort. The quicker they can find their automobiles and slip away, the better.

Bingo players in this town get to be good buddies. The game has probably created more new friendships since television took care of people visiting neighbors and the dull variety shows on the tube marked the beginning of the end of civility in conversation among families.

Bingo has gotten people outside their homes who haven't been away in years.

According to the heavy woman, it's kept many souls from dying at home and waiting for rigor mortis to start.

And something positive can be said about this people-to-people contact in an era when much of the world has seemingly lost touch.

41

Mrs. Martin: good one goes

They buried a giant of a lady, Mrs. Emeline Martin, in the Martin family plot in a hillside cemetery outside Anderson the other day.

The good soul, who reared two doctor sons and four fine daughters, was just a month shy of her 87th birthday anniversary and just weeks away from Mother's Day, 1986.

After the death of her husband, John B. Martin Sr., in the 1970s, Mrs. Martin and her oldest son, Dr. J. B. Martin Jr., remained on the homeplace and Dr. Martin had a sign on the Liberty highway denoting the mother-son team in the field of livestock and horses.

Mrs. Martin, the former Emeline Whitaker, had her tonnage of work, but she did it well.

Her house was more than that. It was a home and there are all too few homes these days.

She died peacefully in Anderson Memorial Hospital after slipping into a coma, according to her physician, Dr. James Bleckley, a member of Internal Medical Associates of Anderson, a facility founded by Dr. J. B. Martin Jr.

"She was a great, good woman," said Dr. Bleckley, who treated her since his arrival in Anderson in 1963.

At the funeral in McDougald's Chapel on North Main Street in Anderson, the Rev. J. W. McKinney spoke of the good times and experiences at the Martin farm.

All the children were there — Dr. J. B. Martin Jr., a younger brother, Dr. Henry Martin, and the three surviving daughters — Doris of Columbia, Becky of Florida, and Eleanor of Anderson. Eleanor had spent many hours with her mother when the doctor sons could not be by her side.

Eleanor consoled and comforted — and that helped immensely in Mrs. Martin's final earthly days.

A fourth daughter, Peg, died in North Carolina some time ago.

Most of the associates of Dr. J. B. and Dr. Henry Martin were present at the funeral, including Dr. Bleckley and another associate, Dr. John D. Ware. The fifth internal medicine specialist, Dr. William Walker, was on call at the hospital and filling in for the other four.

Many nurses and department heads from Anderson Memorial attended services and burial on a knoll out from the farm.

Mrs. Emiline Martin touched numerous lives in her almost 87 years on earth, and she contributed much.

Her five children, 12 grandchildren, and 13 great-grand-children will continue her mission.

And it is comforting to know this good lady spent her first Mother's Day in Heaven with her own mother.

And that is what life and death are all about.

'I just had to come back'

Izzie Russell is a big, black, good woman with a heart of gold and she was back in Red Hill the other day looking over the home where she worked for years.

Izzie and Mom were big buddies, and Izzie spent eight or 10 years helping Mom with the cooking and the ironing and household chores.

Izzie's health failed about the time Mom got worse and she moved to Athens to be with her ailing son and to attend church services as often as she could. Another good lady named Joyce Bennett from Toccoa spent the final two years with Mom and was with her almost until she died in 1984. Joyce was killed in a tragic auto accident the day after Christmas.

Izzie, called "Big Mama" by her large family of children, has not had an easy life. She lost one son in the military, buried another from an auto accident and her husband died after a long illness.

Mom and Izzie talked a lot when Izzie would spend the day at the house. They spoke about their own days of growing up in the large families because Mama was one of 11 children and considered the most sickly, yet outlived all the others.

They spoke of the Bible and church and goodness, and they laughed a lot when one or the other got interested in a soap opera on television.

Those days of Mom and Izzie were good days, and Izzie knew where just about everything was in the big house at Red Hill.

The other day, Izzie returned to that house with her daughter, Betty, and Izzie helped sort out some of the valuables as best she could. She has arthritis in her hands, and they bother her a lot.

"Could I have?....." she said, pausing.

"What, Izzie?"

"Could I have that flower in the window?" she went on. "I'd like something to remember your mama with."

We told the family friend to choose anything she wishes and she selected a kitchen stool both had used for a long time, a mop, a lamp that burned brightly through many a cold and hot night in Red Hill, and Izzie took some shoes we had worn over the years for her son, Carvie. He has big feet too.

"I loved your mother," she said, big tears welling up in her eyes. "And you may not know it, but I'll soon be going where she is. I'm 75 years old, and I never thought I'd make that."

We hugged right there in the kitchen, where there had been so many good meals and great times.

Izzie, who just "had to come back" was home one more time.

The oath YOUR doctor took

A lady in Athens sent a scrawled message on the back of a postcard.

She posed this question: "A few years ago, you wrote something about an oath a doctor takes. I saved mine, but lost it. Could you "run" it again?"

Ma'am, we will be delighted.

Your family physician, the one who supposedly knows all about your physical ills, took what is known as "The Oath of Hippocrates" before he was licensed to practice medicine.

Here it is, the Oath of Hippocrates, taken by your physician, taken by ours.

"Swear by Apollo The Physician, and Aosculapius, and Health, and All-Heal, and all the gods and goddesses, that, according to my ability and judgement, I will keep this oath and this stipulation —

"To reckon him who taught me this art equally dear to me as my parents, to share my substance with him, and relieve his neces-

44

sities if required, to look upon his offspring in the same footing as my brothers, and to teach them this art, if they wish to learn it, without fee or stipulation, and that by precept, lecture, and every other mode of instruction, I will import a knowledge of the art of my own sons, and those of my teachers and to disciples bound by a stipulation and oath according to the law of medicine, but to none others.

I will follow that system of regiment, which, according to my ability and judgment, I consider for the benefit of my patients, and, abstain from whatever is deleterious and mischievous.

I will give no deadly medicine to anyone if asked nor suggest any such counsel and in like manner I will not give to a woman a possary to produce abortion.

With purity and with holiness, I will pass my life and practice my art, I will not cut persons laboring under this stone, but will leave this to be done by men who are practitioners of this work.

Into whatever houses I enter, I will go into them for the benefit of the sick, and will abstain from every voluntary act of mischief and corruption, and further from the seduction of females or males, or free man and slaves.

Whatever, in connection with my professional practice, or not in connection with it, I see or hear, in the life of men, which ought not to be spoken abroad, I will not divulge as reckoning that all such should be kept secret.

While I continue to keep this oath unviolated, may it be granted to me to enjoy life and the practice of art, respected by all men, in all times, but should I trespass and violate this oath, may the reverse be my lot."

Battery-powered radio —1923 style!

The first battery-powered radio sets, referred to in your column, came along about 1923 to our area.

I remember quite well the excitement in Homer, Ga., when the first radio came. It was purchased by several people from Alton Hood of Commerce. Word spread fast that Mr. Hood was in town to install the new radio when he arrived.

A large pole was raised behind Howard Hill's Store for one end of the aerial. Hood then climbed a large tree, which is still standing, across U.S. 441 and attached the other end of the wire.

The radio was about the size of a carpenter's metal tool box and had more dials, knobs, and switches than the Space Shuttle Discovery.

Hill stayed at the controls all the time and would pass the earphone around the crowds to listen to KDKA, Pittsburgh, WLS, Chicago, and WLW, Cincinnati.

It wasn't too long before more stations came on the air, and a loudspeaker was installed. This took the place of the earphone and a lot of confusion about whose turn it was to listen quieted down.

First artists on WSM, Nashville, I can recall were Uncle Dave Macon, DeFord Bailey, and the Fruit Jar Drinkers. DeFord played the fox chase on the French harp. Uncle Dave Macon had a song, "Doris."

Battery-powered radios stayed around Homer until 1936 when Georgia Power came in from Maysville and illuminated Homer. They were not phased out until the early 1940s when REA came along to all the outlying areas.

Toccoa Falls Institute had a radio station in 1929. It was WTFI. The station was sold and moved to Athens. The call letters were still WTFI, and the station was in the Costa Building, now the police station.

Yes, I can remember the Joe Louis fights, also the Tunney-Dempsey fights.

Spare, fully-charged batteries were always on hand. Sometimes, the old Model T or Model A was pulled up close to the windows and wires attached to the battery for power just in case.

Memories, memories.

Sincerely, Bill Gillespie, Commerce.

What's wrong in medical market?

The picture is not bright on the legitimate drug scene in the realm of drugs for depression and the stomach, this column has learned through reliable sources.

There are several cases in point.

The Food and Drug Administration ordered the withdrawal from the market of an anti-depressant pill which allegedly killed several people in Europe. It only found its way to a few Northeast Georgia homes.

And, now a highly-touted drug, Wellbutrin, produced by Burroughs-Wellcome Company in Research Triangle Park, N.C., has been taken off the market.

The drug, which had eight pages of advertising in the March issue of the *AMA Journal,* was supposed to "help patients who cannot tolerate the anticholingeric side effects of alternative treatments."

And the literature promised it would "help patients rediscover the beauty of life."

We placed a telephone call Thursday to Burroughs-Wellcome in North Carolina and talked with Kathy Bartlett of the marketing department.

She was most helpful and quite candid.

"What happened is we voluntarily withdrew the drug in early March after the advertising had been placed," she said. "New data came to light that a study showed four of 50 persons with bulimia, an eating disorder, had seizures while taking the drugs in clinical trials.

Nearly 60,000 bottles, each containing 100 Wellbutrin, had been distributed to wholesalers and retail pharmacies in preparation for the start, were voluntarily withdrawn by our company until the bulimia study had been analyzed and implications considered," said Ms. Bartlett.

That's as honest as a company can be.

She also referred us to an official with the Food and Drug Administration, but he has not returned the call.

While the controversy had been swirling about the two anti-depressant medications, a long-time prescribed drug, Combid, given to people with stomach problems, was quietly removed from the market.

Combid, on the market for perhaps 25 years, had the blessings of many physicians in Northeast Georgia and Western South Carolina.

"The only reason I can give why the FDA took it off the market is that it is a combination drug," said one pharmacist. "The FDA seems to be removing a lot of them, although they have proved beneficial and effective."

The point that doesn't add up is why the Food and Drug Administration seems intent on sticking to the letter, and beyond, on prescribed drugs and will permit a variety of stores to sell over-the-counter merchandise and products without any sort of question.

What do we believe about medicines in 1986?

It's enough to cause wholesale depression!

Clemson, by way of Lavonia

Lavonia has as many University of Georgia football fans per foot as any other community in Georgia.

And Andy Hill, an attorney, would certainly be listed as a number one booster.

That will be verified today when Andy and his wife, Peggy, host an 11 a.m. barbecue at their Lavonia home.

The Hills expect to host about 40 persons, including attorneys and judges and football fans in general, for the big match in Death Valley at Clemson today.

A poem was penned by Andy — or Peggy — and it's timely to publish it this morning — only hours before the match-up.

Keep in mind that Lavonia sits on the South Carolina line and is on the way from Athens to Clemson.

The Hills titled their literary effort: "A Poem?"

It goes like this:

"Another two years have come and gone,
And though we hate to admit it,
We've certainly gotten "older but wiser"?
Forget it!

"One thing never changes though;
You know what we mean —
July is just a warm-up time
For the Bulldog "rootin" team!
"Get out those coolers, red shirts and pins;
Count out those tickets; call up your friends.
Dust off those tail gates; fill up the tanks;
Practice your cheers; send up your thanks!
"August will quickly be over
And then — Glory to the day!
Georgia will play Alabama,
Labor — the Athens way!!
"Next will come good ole Baylor;
Then we'll be on the road:
Clemson — by way of Lavonia —
At last — the cause of this ode!
"Our traditional barbecue welcomes
Those Bulldogs (south, east and west)
who promise to get their own tickets
and be our honored guests.
"Stop by on your way 'cross the river"
We'll greet you with a cool one.
Then fill up your plate and your tummy,
and hop on the bus when you're done!
"The date is September, the 21st
The hour is 11 a.m.
Your hosts are Peggy and Andy Hill
Kick-off is 3 p.m."

Bill Anderson returns to remember

Bill Anderson, the super-successful songwriter, Grand Ole Opry star, Po Folks restaurant advertising spokesman, Fandango host and Nashville producer, came "home" to Northeast Georgia Saturday night.

Home to where it all started.

Home to the return of the memory bank.

Home to the turf he knew so well and conquered so fast in the 1950s.

Home to the people who still trust him, believe him and love him.

Home.

He drove up in a rental Lincoln outside the WNEG-TV, channel 32, studios in Toccoa a little past 6:30 and remained until almost midnight.

The grandson of the late Athens-Elberton Methodist District Superintendent Horace S. Smith brought videos from his game shows and clips from old TV shows and strummed a borrowed guitar from Earl Alexander and had the time of his 47-year-old life for a three-hour, on-the-air live appearance.

Two doctors in the studio audience, Dr. Max Kent, an orthopedic surgeon, and Dr. Kenneth Smith, dermatologist, both of Anderson, S.C., said Bill seemed totally relaxed.

But they knew he was in agony to a degree off camera with a recurring back ailment. The young man has been under severe stress the last year. His devoted wife, Becky, suffered severe injuries in an auto accident almost a year ago; and Bill stayed by her bedside for weeks.

He has been father and mother to their seven-year-old son, Jamey, and the man who used to be a night person sometimes retires as early as 8 p.m., after helping the son prepare for school. He awakens at dawn to get him to class.

Bill Anderson was home though, and he was happy. Roy and Evelyn Gaines of the TV station had hosted the crew, Bill and visitors at a meal prepared by Bill and Helen Chandler of Commerce, Bill's adopted hometown. Bill and all the others dined heavily on fried chicken, roast beef and other delicacies.

Before the show, Bill talked with friends and shook hands with Tom Grant of the Nashville Network and Jerry Farmer of the J&J Center in Athens.

Bill talked about the origin of "Still," his signature song in country music.

Fifteen years ago, Bill said no one would ever know what prompted him to write the tune, "Think I'll Go Somewhere and Cry Myself to Sleep." He declined to expand Saturday night, but he did a verse and chorus.

He also sang "Five Little Fingers," "City Lights," "Po Folks" and "I Love You Drops."

Many of his friends from Commerce and Ila, Dock and Ralph, telephoned the show and Bill reminisced about the pair, along with R.L. and Bonnie Jordan of Commerce.

He talked of his days of WJJC and of his presence at the station when it signed on the air. He remembered his afternoon record shows with "Josh," the duck, and his regard for peanut butter and how the people in the Commerce area had the post office smelling like peanuts at one time.

Bill closed the show with the hymn, "I Can Do Nothing Alone."

Then, suddenly, it was over.

Bill Anderson, king of the hills in Northeast Georgia for 30 years, was back home Saturday night and savoring every minute.

A musical genius and mental giant made a night that will go down in history.

And, if his appearance proved anything, it is that man can come home again!

The press: enough is enough

There was a refreshing sidewalk scene in the mountain town of Dahlonega the other afternoon: A young girl in pigtails selling the latest issue of *Grit* to passersby.

It was more than free enterprise in a fine hour, but we're glad the people at *Grit* are still peddling their news product.

All these years, the weekly publication, which once sold for a nickel, has had the highest journalistic ideals.

The paper stuck to the facts as much as possible — without a lot of sensationalism, and much name-dragging through headlines over and over and over.

Grit printed pictures of America's leaders in conversation with counterparts from other lands and offered offbeat news stories from places like Angola, Ind., or Paris, Tex., or Bangor, Me.

Oh, it had its serialized stories — the fiction. Good, clean fiction in the 1940s, 1950s and 1960s.

We presume the content of *Grit* hasn't changed a whole lot. They've gone to full-process color, and each front page is dominated by attractive pictures.

Some of the modern-day so-called journalism people would take a good cue from the writers of solid publications like *Grit*, those which have endured the good and the bad.

It is too bad that some of our kind in journalism tend to replay the bad as many times as Howard Cosell likes to replay the action on Monday night football.

This bit of "replay after replay" gets boring after a while and we personally resent the fact some of our own can't let the people rest for a change.

We said as much during the Richard Nixon era — when the Washington press castigated the man more than anyone we've known.

What he allegedly did was recorded month after month, year after year, and even to this day that judge with the peculiar name seems obsessed by Richard Nixon.

Closer home, some press people like to "bear down" on personalities in retread after retread after retread.

Enough is enough is enough. In newspapering or anything else.

Our American people deserve to know what's going on, but we should get better than stories heaped upon stories on people who have suffered enough!

Just how good are polls?

It must be an election year. Pollsters are coming out under the employ of television stations and making headlines in the daily press from Rabun Gap to Tybee Light and saying one candidate is ahead of another by 18 percentage points.

Hogwash!

Polls are not worth the amount of electricity required to operate a fancy computer.

The sad part is some people believe everything they see, read or hear, and that includes polls; and some of mankind will go with the winner and drop from the loser's role in a half South Georgia second.

That is the trouble with polls.

For instance, have you been polled this year? Has someone asked you whether or not you will vote for Mattingly or Fowler?

The answer, even without hearing from you, is a loud, resounding no.

Then, who is interviewed, or in other words, pollsters are questioning whom about the candidates?

The answer is they are sampling 40 or 400 people in the Atlanta metro area — and no one knows what sector of the city is involved.

The end result is a poll published in every major newspaper — and the readers aren't told anything about the random selecting of the persons interviewed. And the damage is done once the papers hit the streets.

What it amounts to is the TV station is seeking to improve its ratings by stepping forward with alleged results of a professional pollster.

And that professional pollster is standing with his back pockets filled with money for his so-called expertise.

In past years, some political scientists have proven that polls were engineered by candidates of the past.

Polls aren't the only inexact method of finding out what isn't happening.

Ratings of TV networks are just as hyped. Also hyped are some records which wind up in number one positions in major magazines. The reasons for the alleged success of a network or a particular record could well be the result of the flush of big money.

You don't think so?

Well, you haven't been around the smoke-filled back rooms of some politicians, king-makers, and record promoters.

Polls and ratings are so much hype here in the so-called modern '80s.

If you want to know about polls, you could ask Harry Truman, if he were still around. Or Thomas E. Dewey, a man the polls predicted would flatten Truman.

Truman went to bed thinking he had been defeated, and Dewey retired thinking he was the next president of the United States.

The positive point to make on this Monday — weeks before the November election — is that the only poll that counts is the one that involves you and the privacy of that voting booth.

You have far more power than a money-inspired poll.

Our mom's day is today

Most sons and daughters throughout America will salute their moms Sunday, Mother's Day.

Our tribute is one day early to a precious mama named Pearl Dilworth. She left us on this earthly travail about 3 a.m. Tuesday in the intensive care section of Anderson Memorial Hospital, but she was conscious through it all.

In her weeks-long struggle to live, a battle measured by the will to live, she remained ever-alert, always concerned about others, and acknowledged she didn't feel well.

Mama was a fighter. She told us two days earlier she was putting up a battle.

"But it's rough," she said weakly.

She was the last of 11 children and considered the most sickly of all by Grandma and Grandpa Davis. She outlived them all and attained the 84 figure and would have been 85 on June 8.

One of her nieces, Imogene McCollum of Commerce, had planned a big birthday party at her Lake Hartwell home.

"If I'm here," Mama added.

Mama was concerned about the sick in Red Hill and was stunned to hear the news of Cecil Hunt's fatal heart attack. She grieved with the family of Nellie Frederick, who is battling a 15-year war with leukemia, and losing.

The death of Max, the German Shepherd given to her by Dr. Roy O. McClain, set her back a few days because Max was her guard. He was the best barker in all of Red Hill, and they knew each other's signals.

Now, both are gone.

This morning, we will walk the last earthly mile with Mama after the preachers tell about the goodness of this woman — a lady who never had any bad habits, never talked about people and always had something kind to say about everyone.

And we're going to let you in on a secret this morning.

The newspapering of Billy Dilworth did not start from the pen of the bashful 14-year-old when he pounded a typewriter for the Red Hill News in the *Lavonia Times*. It was written in long-hand by Pearl Dilworth with Billy Dilworth's byline.

"I can't keep this up for you," she said after the fourth week. "If that's going to be your career, you must do it yourself."

She wrote some fine columns, and one of these days we will reprint a couple. She kept up with who was visiting whom and how they got there.

Her mind, even until death, was sharp as a tack, and she was interested in the welfare of the families of her Anderson doctors.

She asked Dr. John Martin and Dr. Henry Martin about their mother, who is 12 days older than Mama. She asked Dr. Jimmy Bleckley about his family and inquired the same from Dr. Max Kent — even as she lay tubed, isolated and insulated from loved ones in that place they call intensive care.

The preachers can't say too much about this good woman. She lived her life fully, better than 1,019 months.

When they silence the Saturday radio show for an hour this morning between 11 and noon on WLET-Radio in Toccoa, the announcers will be playing church music — sacred music, songs of faith. We wouldn't dare exploit commercialism as we bury this giant of a woman.

The walk to the grave from Allens Methodist Church will be as difficult as that long walk nine years ago, when we said an earthly goodbye to Dad, another Christian man and father.

The steps will be difficult to take, but knowing that friends from all walks of life will be walking the real estate with us will help ease the pain.

Happy Mother's Day, Mom, up in Heaven.

You're a day earlier than the rest of all the moms in this country, but you've always been shy about getting your name in the paper on your birthday or a special deal.

This time, Mom, you deserve your day.

Tell Dad hello and tell him a son will follow you to the clouds and Heaven one of these days.

The other night, at 9 p.m. in intensive care, we told you goodnight.

Good day, Mama... and if God needs any good writers in that great Newsroom In the Sky, you'll do just fine.

Today: flowers for Mama

In some respects, many days have been overly stressed in this world of commercialism and much-ado-about-nothing.

No one is exempt, really. The businesses promote special sales to hear the cash registers ring and people in advertising pump the same merchandise for a similar purpose — a good bottom-line figure.

Much of this is blatantly wrong. A special day for baseball, football, basketball, track, special drives.

However, one day, Mother's Day, this very day, deserves every kind of recognition all of us can muster.

A country singer wrote "Flowers for Mama" and detailed how he bought flowers for his own mother and took them to her personally after he saw a young boy kneeling by his mother's grave and heard the boy talking to his mother.

"I talk to her every day," C. W. McCall says of the young boy speaking to the woman in the ground.

Moms deserve recognition. Now, and in the hereafter.

People used to wear red roses in honor of their living moms, and some still do.

Others wore white flowers in memory of their deceased mothers.

Some of the world has gotten away from that, and this is not a good sign in 1980 — a time period taken over more by yellow ribbons and hostages than red roses and caring about the woman who dried you when you were wet as a kid, bathed you in cool water when you raged with fever in sickness.

There will be some children who will make their once-a-year-trips to see their mothers on this day. They appreciate this, of course, but it should be more than a once-a-year affair.

The real tragedy is that situation where children won't visit their mothers today or any day.

Jimmy Dean summed it up well in a hit tune years ago called, "I.O.U."

"Mom, I owe you a lot," he said on record. "For worrying, for caring, for loving."

Mom, we do owe you a lot.

Thank you for providing clean clothes.

Thank you for not chewing us out every day we walked into the house with a dirty shirt after playing softball or football or basketball all Sunday afternoon.

Thank you for the hot biscuits on a cold winter morn.

Thank you for the iced tea in the cotton fields on a hot summer afternoon.

Thank you for taking us to church on Sunday morning and Sunday night.

Thank you for helping us spell because you always liked spelling and grammar.

Most of all, thank you for being Mom.

We could write from now until the end of time and not offer the fitting words.

Happy Mother's Day, Mom.

Friends ease sorrow and depression

This piece is difficult to compose.

The first day back to school after a long summer's absence was tough enough, but the first hour at the typewriter after the traumatic loss of an 84-year-old mom is rough indeed.

These last two weeks, even three months, have taken their toll, but the Good Lord doesn't place more on His people than they can endure.

We keep saying that silently and publicly, and the answer comes back with the knowledge that friends by the tons are helping.

Her funeral was attended by hundreds of friends and family. There is an immediate family of just one — and that thought struck home when we pulled in front of the funeral home in Lavonia that night and the sign read "for immediate family only."

Friends. They helped in many ways.

Dr. Max Kent, the orthopaedic surgeon and Dr. Ken Smith, the dermatologist, both of Anderson, stood by like brothers. Dr. Kent joined Otto McDonald, Gene and Irene Bollinger of WLET Radio, Toccoa, when we went to Commerce to purchase a suit for the funeral.

Dr. Smith and his wife, Linda, sat by our side as the immediate family.

Friends. They go beyond the call of duty.

Four nights were spent in Greenville, S.C., with Mama's nephew, Fred Davis, his wife, Ruby, and their son, Bobby.

They tried to keep us busy. Allen Power asked us to watch the West Coast country music awards from Hollywood, Calif., and there was Kenny Rogers live from Smithsonia on national TV.

Dining out the first night in Greenville, we ran into Grady Peck and his wife, of Toccoa. Grady and Dad were fast friends and Grady is a Monday night regular at the wrestling matches and the lady at the cash register knows the couple's first names.

Allen Power carried us to the Robert Redford movie, *The Natural*, and it helped, but there is a story in the movie that threads and hurts.

Friends. They endured.

Donald and Janie Hamby and their son, Steve, of Lavonia, welcomed us into their house for three nights and one night, Friday, was spent at the Steak and Ale Restaurant in Athens marking Steve's 17th birthday anniversary.

Thursday and Friday, the first days back in Georgia, were rough, and almost unbearable.

The Saturday radio show was difficult, the internal medicine specialist, Dr. John Martin, said getting back into harness was the best therapy. He's probably right.

Dr. Robert Sullivan of Carnesville listened, along with his wife, June. They invited us in their home Sunday, Mother's Day, and we talked about a variety of things.

The newspaper people, Robert Chambers and Hank Johnson and Melvin Epps and Tom Travin and Mike Childs, have been supportive, and all the people at the radio station in Toccoa, Otto and Betty, Hiram and Beth, Gene and Irene, have been in there helping too.

Ross and Barbara Cloer of Mountain City have opened their doors this week and the lady who looked after Mama the last year, Mrs. Joyce Bennett of Toccoa, has tried to keep the house going in Red Hill. Robert Franklin and Robert Macomson, neighbors, have helped too.

This piece would not be complete without thanking hundreds of people for flowers, the friends and neighbors for the food they kept on our tables, the preachers who comforted, the hundreds of sympathy cards still pouring in each day.

An 89-year-old lady, named Davis, who lives alone in Athens, wrote a long letter expressing sympathy and wondered if Mama's daddy was named Will and lived in Lavonia. His name was William and he did, indeed, live there and died there.

A cousin from Elberton wrote a 13-page letter and relayed how the pastor of her Methodist church read the column, "Today Is Our Mom's Day," in the church worship service on Mother's Day.

Lt. Gov. and Mrs. Zell Miller drove from Atlanta to pay respects, along with Mrs. Mary Beazley, long-time executive secretary to President Jimmy Carter. Mrs. Beazley's parents, the Hunter Wilsons of Decatur, were among Mama and Daddy's best friends when Wilson was principal at Red Hill Junior High School.

People we haven't seen in years came, but the ladies of Allens Methodist outdid themselves preparing food at the house for hundreds that day.

Bill Anderson telephoned; his parents, Mr. and Mrs. Jim Anderson of Decatur, attended the funeral, and we heard from people we haven't seen in years.

Friends. They stand by you in a crisis.

Janet Callahan, secretary of the newspaper office in Lavonia, worked many overtime hours during the past few weeks during illness, then death. Joel and Shirley Shirley helped with conversation.

Cotton Carrier and Jane, long-time stars of "TV Ranch" on WAGA-TV, came to the funeral and to the house. Mama had cooked several meals for the TV Wranglers when they were sponsored by the church's youth group and admission to the show was 30 and 60 cents.

The Saturday mail brought a letter from the Smith brothers, Tennessee and Smitty. They had better harmony on Atlanta TV than the Wilburn or the Louvin Brothers, but they chose to stay in Atlanta TV.

Wilbur Fitzgerald, Atlanta lawyer turned actor, was there, and funeral home owners John Hurley of Athens and James Neal of Toccoa, were there with messages of sympathy.

A state trooper, Jim Ledford, attached to the Toccoa patrol post, along with Franklin County deputies, directed traffic before and after the funeral and Ledford was off duty because he had worked the night before.

Three ladies in white, Mrs. Dot Smith and Mrs. Edna Morris of Anderson and Mrs. Pat McCollum of Hartwell stood by her side night and day.

Dr. Jimmy Bleckley, Jr., of Clayton, member of the Martin, Bleckley, Walker, and Ware team, and the last doctor to treat Mama, inked a powerful message. He said, "I guess we all go through a stage where we think we will live forever and we tend to overlook that Death is a part of life's process. It's been hard for me to accept this concept also....

"Thinking of you and I love you," he concluded.

In death, there is irony.

Earl Alexander of Alto spent the two weeks by our side during Mama's illness in Anderson. Dr. Ken Smith had given the use of his Anderson home.

And just last Saturday afternoon, Earl's own mama died in Groveland, Fla. He leaves tomorrow on that long road in our car to pay final respects to that dear soul who had been unconscious for two years.

Sunday night, Earl joined us in evening worship at Hill's Crossing Baptist Church near Clarkesville.

The new pastor, the Rev. Eugene A. Power, father of Allen Power, had us for lunch that day and his Sunday night sermon launched a week-long revival that runs through this Friday night.

His message, "Is anything too hard for the Lord?" was comforting for two men who lost their best earthly friends in a span of a little more than a week.

The preacher talked of God's 30,000-plus promises in the Bible and stressed "there is no problem too big for God to handle."

"There is no place too hard for God to survive," he said. "God is still in the soul-saving business."

They ended the service with the old-time hymn, "Lord, I'm Coming Home."

That song had more meaning and depth than ever....

Friendship: six big marks

True friends, those who stick closer than brothers — well, they've all been seemingly scarce lately. And in an era troubled at home by the economy, internationally by jealous strife.

That's why Dr. Roy O. McClain's sermon on friendship was appropriate the other day at Orangeburg First Baptist Church in the South Carolina city.

The good preacher was forthright, saying that four-fifths of his own congregation, or any congregation, cannot go the extra mile on a friend's behalf.

"This ought not be," he said, "in an age of the mania-for-more and rip-offs on every turn."

The minister, whose column appears on the church pages of Saturday, measured six marks of true friendship:

- One who guards you when you're not on guard.
- One who commends you when you're right.
- One who rebukes you when you're wrong.
- One who does not desert you when you're in trouble.
- One who knows all about you and still likes you.
- One who would lay down his life for you if need be.

All are powerful points, and consider them carefully.

Dr. McClain went into detail on each in his 20-minute sermon, and he told his congregation a true friend does not turn his back when one is in trouble.

"Even if it means that friend's in jail," he said.

His final point was strong too.

"I have a friend who gave His life for me, and for you," the preacher said. "His name is Jesus Christ. And I've never seen Him, but I am going to see Him one day. That's what friendship is all about."

Our day needed a sermon like that.

Where does church stand today?

All sorts of goodie-type topics arise at family get-togethers and one of them took place the other Sunday at the home of Sammy J. Beggs in the Gold Mine Community of Hart County and revolved around the church.

There were three ministers present — two Baptists and one Methodist — and one of them wondered out loud in response to lay questions about people who depend on song books for hymns they've sung for 40 or 50 years.

"Then they're some of the ones who get concerned because the preacher reads the sermon," the minister said. Good point.

We first brought up the subject of American church-goers who sing from the famous hymn books used since oldtimers were kids.

You know the songs. Hymns like, "Rock of Ages," "Have Thine Own Way, Lord," and "Standing on the Promises."

They're all great songs and tremendous hymns of the church, but virtually 100 percent of the people who sing in church have, through habit, continued to refer to hymnals for each word of the song — although the same songs have been sung Sunday after Sunday, lo these many years.

Why and what's the prognosis?

The "why" is easy to answer. It's just that human beings, being human, apparently haven't learned the lines from the old songs, and they know the book is handy anyway.

The prognosis brings on a different sort of analysis, however.

We doubt that tomorrow's generation will improve over today's in reciting songs rather than memorizing them.

One of the preachers said he's concerned over the more important question of how many realize the words they sing.

Someone else suggested the congregation might remember a minister's sermon only a few minutes.

That caused some headshaking. In an age of bombardment by everything the imagination can fathom via the television and radio, it isn't staggering anymore that Americans must refer to the Baptist hymnal or the Methodist hymnal to sing "All Hail the Power of Jesus' Name."

The positive point to make is that absorbing it through repetition must be vastly better than not hearing the songs at all.

Meet J. Alton Wingate— an innovator in banking

The sun had not been up a half hour when the pleasant man in his 50's drove his white Lincoln Town Car into a parking lot at Community Bank & Trust in Cornelia, and he was exactly on time for a promised interview.

Two nights before, J. Alton Wingate was pursuing banking in Pittsburg, Penn., and here he was back in Habersham County looking after a multitude of challenges that brought him to the forefront in banking.

Mr. Wingate is known as a world innovator in banking — 1996 style — for reasons many-fold.

Mr. Wingate's story reads like a fairy tale, and is as true to life as dawn and sunset.

The son of the late James Leonard and Ida Lois Hatcher Wingate of Albany in deep south Georgia, this banker, a public relations wizard par excellence, started his business career at a tender age. In his teens, as a youngster who grew up on a farm, he got his baptism by fire running a newspaper route for the *Albany Herald*, owned by the Gray family, and a route he ran for seven years. He will never forget his editor, a man named James McIntosh.

"I had 625 customers and back then there were very few cars around," Mr. Wingate explained in an interview in the boardroom of Community Bank & Trust the other morning. Sitting at the end of a large table, the down-to-earth businessman said he started his paper route on a bicycle, moved up to a Harley-Davidson motorcycle, and as the route continued to grow, his brother, Stokeley, helped him buy his first car, a 1950 four-door Mercury. He was 17 at the time.

Strange thing about that first job. One of his customers was George Busbee, destined to become the governor of Georgia, but the young J. Alton Wingate didn't know that. However, he remembered the address of the Busbees at 103 NottinghamWay. The paper was 36 cents a week and he made 72 cents a month — what an example he was setting then for the youth of today.

Mr. Wingate had the full support of his parents and remembers growing up on the farm.

When he had the time, he spent spare moments alongside a fence row, where he hunted for birds, sold rabbits trapped in boxes, and also peas and watermelons.

This amazing entrepreneur spent two years of college at Georgia Southwestern in Americus, keeping the paper route at the same time and was involved in Porterfield Memorial Methodist Church. Some of his buddies helped him collect his route on Saturday mornings.

A sister, Veda, was the first banker in the Wingate family and she directed operations for C&S Bank in Albany.

Later, he went to Atlanta to seek a job at C&S, and applied for admission at Georgia State. A man named Cliff Campbell asked him if he would consider staying in Albany at C&S. Mr. Wingate did just that, because the University of Georgia had an extension center in Albany.

In the meantime, he lost his father when he was a senior in high school, and the only person living at home with his mother was an older brother, who has just retired from the composing room at the *Albany Herald.*

Mr. Wingate credits Cliff Campbell, who is now retired and living in Thomasville, with being his mentor in banking.

Although Mr. Wingate had the chance to go to Atlanta, Athens or Valdosta to work at any of the three C&S banks, he elected to go to Athens because of Bob Kimbrell, whom he described as "one of the finest people I have ever met in my life."

Mr. Wingate went to night school at Georgia, worked there until 1966, where his primary responsibility was business development, and this is where he had the opportunity to call on leaders in northeast Georgia, specifically Cornelia, Toccoa, Carnesville, Clarkesville, Elberton, Hartwell, Winder and Madison.

He considers this the doormat that allowed him to get into Habersham County, and some of the first persons he met were Calvin Stovall, Paul Reeves, Howard Wheeler, and Louis Puckett.

One of the best years in many good years for this man occurred in 1964, when he met Linda Hodgkinson, who had worked as a secretary at the bank in Athens, and served as his temporary secretary for a time.

Mr. Wingate is proud of his family — his devoted wife and son, Beau, who is with Financial Supermarket, Frank and Edward. Frank lives in Greenville, S.C., and launched Community Bank of Greenville in the South Carolina city. Edward lives in Nashville, Tenn., and is in electronics. They have three grandchildren, Caroline — four years old, Meredith — two and one half, and Anna Lea — one.

The Wingates moved to Cornelia in 1966 and are marking their 30th year in Habersham County.

"I consider myself to be one of the luckiest bankers in the state. Also, I was lucky enough to come to a town like Cornelia and Habersham," Mr. Wingate said.

He began to see in the 70s that the banking industry was going through tremendous changes, and since Cornelia Bank had been around since 1900, and being a smaller institution in a smaller community, this gave him the opportunity to see, deal and touch the marketplace.

In 1977, Mr. Wingate became president and CEO, and soon learned the bank needed to diversify, allowing them to have other resources to draw upon.

The assets of the old bank were 30 million dollars when he

took over. Today's assets of the Community Bank & Trust are a whopping 300 million dollars.

Mr. Wingate said there are about 429 owners, with employees as major stockholders. "We elected to do a 30-for-1 split in December 1995, and our shareholders were delighted, because we had never had a stock split," he continued.

Charles McKellar heard his version of supermarket banking when he lived in Charlotte. Mr. Wingate said, "Today, we are able to put together the largest instore banking program in the world, and brought Winn-Dixie and Nations Bank together for the first time in Florida, and Nations Bank will be going into 240 Winn-Dixie stores there. That was one of the highlights of my life to bring the fifth largest supermarket and the fifth largest financial institution together, plus the fact that we were here in Cornelia, Ga."

He credits Howard Hess, Sr., Vice President and Regional Director, for Winn-Dixie as a key supporter and friend, and one who taught him the supermarket business.

In 1996, Mr. Wingate has placed supermarket banks in 20 states, and predicts more new ventures by the year 2000.

A veritable ball of energy, this banking legend logs 20,000 miles a year on his car, 300,000 by air, and wishes he could get Jim Tatum at Habersham County airport to give him credit for the number of hours they have spent together in a plane.

"I am awfully fortunate to have people like Calvin Stovall, chairman of the holding company; and Annette Fricks, who works a minimum of 12 hours a day, and who has been my secretary for all but six months in 30 years," Mr. Wingate said.

He will tell you in a flash that many people are responsible for his success — folks like Mr. Campbell, Mr. Kimbrell, Mr. Stovall and Mr. Reeves, who, he said, "was a very good customer of mine at C&S, as well as a close friend, even though he was at a competing bank. He is a super guy."

Mr. Wingate is, indeed, proud of Cornelia First United Methodist Church, which is an important part of his life. He said the church committed itself to spending in excess of a million dollars in a building program. As of the first of August 1996, only an indebtedness of $28,000 remained, and, last month the note was burned and the church is debt-free.

By 2000, Mr. Wingate said he would like to be doing an even better business than he is today. He thinks supermarket banking will grow even faster, and notes the most distant location is a facility in Metz, France.

From paper boy to a former governor in south Georgia, to a leader in banking and supermarket banking in much of North America, this 56-year-old financial wizard is continuing to blaze new trails.

Remembered: days of '50s

Charles Kuralt made a lot of us who were teenagers in the era of the 1950s remember in his two-hour special on TV.

In fact, the "On the Road" specialist for CBS-TV outdid himself with his presentation of kinescope recordings from some of the early shows on television.

He had the late Edward R. Murrow puffing on his famous cigarette and talking about new gadgetry and pioneering with remote-control television camera on a show called "Person to Person."

He had Douglas Edwards, still with CBS, looking awfully young and trim and reading the news back in 1951.

There was the late John Charles Daly also reading the news — this time on ABC. But he missed a good one in not pulling from the files one of the "What's My Line" shows when Daly told one of the panel members who missed identifying a guest, "Let's flip the cards and give the full $50."

There was the host looking very much alive in the much-debated TV game show called "The $64,000 Question."

Eugene McCarthy was holding his congressional hearings and later they were holding some on him.

There were film clips from George Burns and Gracie Allen, and now Gracie has departed and George is still bunting with his cigar.

There were scenes from the old successful shows called "Suspense" on the mystery front and "Howdy Doody" on the fun front.

Kuralt talked about the afternoons being filled with kids' shows and old-time western movies and indicated it looked as though there were creases on the television screen.

We were shown the acceptance speech of Dwight David Eisenhower and the disappointing look of Taft, who had wanted the Republican nomination. Now, both are dead.

He showed us Richard Nixon's speech about "Checkers," his dog, and it depicted how the presidency can age a man.

Kuralt showed Harry Truman when he fired Gen. Douglas McArthur and McArthur when he made his famous statement, "Old soldiers never die...they just fade away..."

He gave us clips of the "Kukla, Fran and Ollie" puppet show and sketches of the late Ed Sullivan. He talked about how the news announcers had no film clips to illustrate their stories and how the newsmen would get up and walk around and sit on the corner of their desk just to show action.

Charles Kuralt told much about the 1950s — and indicated those indeed were the calm years, particularly after the Korean War.

He said TV started losing money and only one in 109 homes had a television set at the outset of the decade. In another eight years, he reported eight of 10 homes with TV and the industry soaring into profits to the tune of millions of dollars.

Maybe the reason TV is so sorry today is because the networks are depositing advertising money in the banks by billions, and we're worse off and suckers for watching.

A world of spinning wheels

An old-model automobile turned into the parking lot out front of the office the other day, and the driver caused the tires to squeal.

Across the street, at the convenience store, wheels turned and screamed on another car five minutes later.

This business of spinning wheels is getting to be big business, even with the so-called energy crisis and escalating gasoline costs.

But we shouldn't blame the cars or the trucks. The drivers ought to get the real blame.

It wasn't too many years ago when a dear aunt commented about one of her sons getting out of military service after the Korean War.

"Seems like," she said, "after he's been in service, he isn't content staying home anymore."

They called it, we remember, the beginning of the age or restlessness.

We all thought it would end shortly after the war and that frayed nerves would become better and the country would settle down.

But you see what happened.

Modern tranquilizers, with fancy-sounding names, came on the market and kept many a soul out of mental hospitals.

But those same people kept in society, drive cars daily, and all of us join the rat-race of much-ado-about-nothing and the mere spinning of wheels.

Oh, preachers talk about it from the pulpit and often get frenzied in the process and do precious little ministerial guidance other than for 20 minutes on Sunday morning.

Physicians can get in lengthy jaw sessions and describe what's wrong with society, yet spend less than five minutes in a cubicle with a patient and prescribe a product that may or may not help.

Politicians get up in the halls and debate what's wrong with the country, but give us little direction toward righting matters.

Counselors spend hours talking about a nation's ills, but cannot unravel their own problems.

Like the cobbler whose shoes are filled with holes and the TV repairman whose own set is on the blink, many of those who are supposed to help the rest spend much time spinning wheels are turning wheels in vain themselves.

Such is life.

And such is life in an era, without hot bullets, but with a constant barrage of wars with words.

Pitts broadcast era is over

Sorry to say, Northeast Georgia's sports radio is not the same this fall.

For more than three decades, Len Pitts called virtually every play-by-play in basketball, football and much of baseball, in counties from Elbert on the south to Rabun on the north, extending into metro Atlanta, and into tournaments in Macon and even below the fall line.

After Mr. Pitts' untimely death at the age of 57, the heir apparent and premier play-by-play announcer was his senior son, Greg Pitts.

The son did his duties well these years after his dad's death, although he must have endured a lot of anguish going to the stadiums and gymnasiums where his dad called every play and knew thousands of people, players, coaches and fans by name.

For better than 41 years, the Pitts tradition has continued in radio.

Until now.

The junior Pitts dutifully served as color man for a broadcast the other night, involving Stephens and Franklin Counties in football — a task he did not relish.

But he did the job with gusto, just to prove he could do it right.

Powers-that-be at WLET-FM in Gainesville abruptly changed gears and told Mr. Pitts that he would be doing color and someone else would be doing play-by-play.

That's about like the cart pulling the horse, sterling going apart from silver, and the announcement that Quaker Oats would not be turning out a product anymore.

What a shocker and what a shame.

The senior Pitts, often with a cigar clenched between his teeth, knew sports inside and out, and his son is just as talented and familiar.

In our 28 years of work with Len Pitts, Greg Pitts would substitute for his father, and many would comment how closely the two resembled in voice and inflection, and how the listener seemed to get a grasp mentally of what was going on.

When Otto McDonald and Hiram McDonald, brothers, owned WLET-FM, the station was in Toccoa, and they had enough business knowledge and common sense to know it takes a known man to provide a good air project.

But the station, which has changed identity several times since the McDonald sale, may have pulled a massive blunder.

It just won't seem like fall without hearing a Pitts voice on the air — telling us Franklin kicked a field goal, Elbert missed a two-pointer, or Stephens was successful in amassing 40 yards in a single play.

It was fun to hear Len Pitts and Greg Pitts. Len Pitts would often tell us on drives back from a game like Danielsville or Monroe, "Yes, I'm proud of Greg, and you don't know how good it makes me feel to know he's taking up where I'm leaving off."

This tradition should not end in 1996, but we thought you listeners should know why the voice of Greg Pitts is not on the airwaves, scattered across the hills and valleys of an area that knows Len Pitts and Greg Pitts as household words.

Phil draws well at Red Hill

Phil Gailey was unaware at the time. He was too busy asking questions of the President of the United States.

But he had good TV ratings in Red Hill Monday night.

Gailey, White House correspondent for the *Washington Star* who has been President Carter's shadow four years now, stood and asked a question at the last news conference, had his name and paper's name flashed on the TV screens all across America, and Red Hill.

And it had to be a big night for the young man from the Silver Shoals precinct of Banks County.

Gailey asked President Carter about reports circulating in Washington over a power struggle between national security advisor Zbigniew Brzezinski and retiring Secretary of State Cyrus Vance.

"That's an erroneous report," Carter responded.

Gailey, with a suit the same color as the President's and with a bow tie, sat down.

He had his moment in history and did well.

His mama, Mrs. Garland Gailey, was watching in Silver Shoals and was obviously proud of her son.

Three hours later, at 12:15 a.m. Tuesday, we talked over the telephone with Gailey in the *Star* newsroom.

"Do you realize there were millions of people looking at you?" we asked.

He paused.

"I guess," he said, "that's the one fringe benefit of this job, where we stay holed in so much of the time."

Gailey seemed pleased he did well in the TV ratings at Red Hill, but he's no dummy. He knew most people couldn't get any other channels but CBS, ABC and NBC. Particularly in a rural area without the modern miracle of a TV cable and where HBO is known as human body odor and nothing similar to that feature in town known as Home Box Office.

Monday night was a big night for Georgians.

Judy Woodruff, who paid her dues at Channel 5 in Atlanta, is now with a national TV network, and, like Gailey and Sam Donaldson, follows President Carter full-time.

And Phil Gailey.

And President Carter.

For a moment under the blazing TV lights there, the circle was complete.

You won't see any nickel hotdogs in 1996

A few things once common, but now seldom seen:
- Free hot lunches in school.
- Three-minute 10-cent long-distance telephone calls.
- A nickel hotdog.

• Human beings who still attend Sunday night church services, as well as Sunday morning services, and there was a time, not so long ago, when Wednesday night services were well attended.

• A $5 per month flat rate light bill.

• Gasoline for the flivver at 25-cents a gallon.

• Politicians who deliver after the election instead of so much verbal hogwash before the polls open.

• Americans who praise their President when he does solid things, as well as offer constructive criticism, rather than spend 90 percent of their time being critical and the other 10 percent being skeptical.

• A new $2,500 car.

• Shuck mops.

• Aladdin lamps.

• 'Possum hunts and beyond that, 'possum suppers, complete with sweet potatoes and other trimmings.

• Women who wear dresses, even short ones, instead of the over-abundance of pantsuits.

• School teachers who can correct unruly school children with a single sentence.

• People who criticize law enforcement officers at the drop of a pin, and then turn around and call them for a favor on a whim.

• The nickel firecracker and 25-cent Roman candle, now outlawed in Georgia, yet it's perfectly legal in this state for someone to fire a double barreled shotgun, rifle or pistol, either of which could kill or maim.

• Lawyers who get accused of saying one thing and then reversing themselves the next minute.

• Genuine peanut brittle.

• Old fashioned hoop cheese.

• The age-old expression, "The family who prays together, stays together."

• Folks who mean what they say and say what they mean.

• Remember when, not long ago, a man's handshake was better than a 20-page contract.

• When television was a happy medium and not one that dwelled on sex, silly talk shows and real comedy, rather than 90 minutes of the kind offered on prime time shows every night, with no subject being sacred.

• Penny candy far bigger than a penny and "guess whats" that had far more suspense for the buyer than an expensive Georgia lottery ticket in the summer of 1996.

• When you get a real telephone call instead of somebody on the other line trying to make a pitch and offering everything from the chance of a lifetime to a change of telephone carriers.

• Good doctors who spend time talking to their patients and listening too.

'She's wearing blanket of stone'

It was like the World Series, Metropolitan Opera, New Year's Eve on Times Square, and the Grand Ole Opry all wrapped in one big package.

Burl Ives, maybe one of the world's best singers ever, captivated a large crowd in the spacious, elevated auditorium at Anderson College here the other night.

But Ives had the rapt attention of everyone when he sang, as his second song after intermission, the international hit, "Mary Ann Regrets."

The audience listened intently as he did the words about the boy from the country in love with the girl from the city and a situation frowned upon by the girl's mother, who objected because the boy was from the "other side of the tracks."

"Mary Ann regrets she'll be unable to see you again, she's leaving for Europe next week and she'll be busy 'til then," he sang.

The song gets sadder.

Ives closed his eyes, then sang, "My Mary Ann died; they say she just wasted away. If I could have seen her, I know she'd be living today. If I could have been there, she'd be wearing my ring stead of a blanket of stone."

Lord, that's tough!

He went through much of his repertoire with songs like "Little Bitty Tear Let Me Down," "Funny Way Of Laughing," and "Blue Tail Fly."

The man talked of his recording session in Nashville 30 years ago and of how the song made radio station lists. One album cut contained a Bill Anderson-penned tune, "Ninety-Nine Years."

The scene was almost sobering as Ives walked tediously, painfully, but methodically, from the side of the stage to his set at mid-stage, where his only props were a chair, and a small table to his right.

The table held a glass of apple juice, which kept his voice steady and a glass of water, which provided moisture.

Most men in their advancing 80s would not be in a college auditorium or any public setting with such simple props.

But Burl Ives is not an average person.

His voice is smooth as silk.

His mind is as sharp as a 25-year-old.

He has the polish of a college professor.

And his stage presence is that of a pro who has paid his dues many times.

"I'm not bashful because I look down," he told the crowd of 500 at one point. "I'm looking at my guitar to see the listing of songs my wife wrote down."

Thankfully, that list included "Mary Ann Regrets..."

And there is that sudden thought—how many other Mary Anns died last night?

Funeral brings back memories, friends

This is where it all started, and one day this is where it will all come to an earthly end.

This time, it was going back to Allens United Methodist Church for the funeral services of J.R. Randall, a neighbor and friend, who died suddenly after battling illness since 1988.

Unbelievably, the obituary said he was 80, but in reality, this good man was still in his 50s in our memory.

It was an uplifting funeral, if funerals can be uplifting, because it was a celebration of life for a man who left a devoted widow, the former Sue Oliver, seven sons and one daughter, a host of grandchildren and great-grandchildren, and two sisters, Nell and Bonnie.

The Rev. C. Roy Smith, a Baptist minister with roots in Gum Log, told the crowd of Mr. Randall's goodness to family and friends, and "you would bank on his word."

The Rev. Herb Blackburn, Allens pastor for more than a year, talked somberly, yet at the same time confidently, of J. R. Randall's relationship with God, with his family, with his church and with his pastor. "One day, when he was so sick at the hospital in Royston, they had a teddy bear in his bed, and family members told me that J. R. called the toy 'Herb,' a compliment indeed."

The good man's friends and neighbors formed the choir to sing two old time hymns, "Take My Hand, Precious Lord" and "Softly and Tenderly."

Finally, at the end of the service, as family and friends and the sons who served as pallbearers filed out, the choir and congregation stood to sing from page 43 in the Cokesbury hymnal, "Amazing Grace."

Going back to this friend's funeral was more than just saying goodbye to another fine soul.

It brought back memories:

Memories of the first funeral we ever attended at Allens at the tender age of four, and tears flowed like a river from mourners over the funeral of, ironically one of Mrs. J. R. Randall's relatives, an Oliver.

J. R. and Sue reared a great family, and we had the opportunity to catch up on conversation with some of the children after the funeral. One of the oldest sons, John, just six years our junior, said he hoped to return to Red Hill to live some day, and maybe Thomas Wolfe can be disproved once more when he wrote the book, *You Can't Go Home Again.*

The memories paraded of saints gone before — of Mr. George Crenshaw, who pioneered in the Sunday school, and whose son, Dr. Hoyt, was one of the outstanding orthopaedic surgeons in Memphis, Tenn.; Mrs. Florrie Ramey, who played the organ and piano, and directed the Methodist Youth Fellowship without a salary of even a dime for years and years, and somehow we never appropriately honored this good lady, who drove a big Buick to church, loaded down with kids, Sunday night after Sunday night, and she kept us in church or some of us might have been in jail otherwise; of Grandmother Dilworth, who died years ago, and who taught Sunday school and whose number one project was getting chimes for the church; of Mr. and Mrs. H. R. LeCroy, who reared a fine family, and Mrs. LeCroy was known for her creative dishes of food that kept quarterly meetings good for the soul and added weight to the preacher and district superintendent, because there was always a ton of fried chicken, fresh corn, fried okra and frostyback pies.

Many in the congregation were friends from bygone years who came to speak to us and shake hands after the funeral, and to welcome us back to Red Hill.

One other deed that should be mentioned was the Sunday the late Mr. and Mrs. J. O. Kelly donated a huge air conditioner system for the church, and we doubt they even had air conditioning in their house — and that was a far cry from the funeral home cardboard fans that pumped the hot air across the face as mourners fanned for their lives at church services and funerals.

Suddenly, Red Hill seemed alive again — with animals making their sounds next to the cemetery at John Adams' home.

In previous years, about this time, Red Hill people would have been talking about the cotton crop, the corn outlook and perhaps what sorghum cane crops might produce. By now, there is no cotton, corn; for the most part, is bought from the grocery store and sorghum syrup can only be found in Blairsville and is even getting scarce there.

It's good to come home to visit and the fact that J. R. Randall's death brought us back to Red Hill this time meant all the folk with local ties went back to them one more time.

But Mr. Randall and the hundreds of folk in graves across from the church in that big cemetery that's getting larger by the year are in a much better place, where they don't worry about crops, droughts, air conditioning or sickness, and even death.

Fletcher Seabolt builds Dairy Queen City

Up in Turner's Corner in Lumpkin County, the big fluffy clouds bump the blue sky in mid-afternoon.

It is here that Fletcher Seabolt first saw the light of day, and the son of the late Mr. and Mrs. Arch Seabolt had never heard of an ice cream twirl in his young life.

But in the decades that followed, the ice cream with the twirl on top was to make Mr. Seabolt the best-known restauranteur in much of the South. In fact, today, the Hartwell Dairy Queen has the fifth largest volume of business in the whole world, a fact that the lean, kind-hearted man has to be pleased about.

One of seven children and the middle son in a family of two boys and five girls, he has lived in Hart County for a quarter century. He purchased the Hartwell Dairy Queen on Friday, the 13th in August of 1971, from Dr. B. J. Davis and Jimmy Lawrence, after hearing about the establishment being on the market from Julian and Robert Westmoreland, when Julian owned the Toccoa Dairy Queen on West Currahee Street, and later built a second on Big A Road in Toccoa. Julian married Mr. Seabolt's sister, Callie, who still lives in Toccoa, and is in real estate.

His first trip to Hartwell was to look at the Dairy Queen and he bought it a week later.

Mr. Seabolt, with a note of sadness in his voice, was happy to say his Dad and Mom lived to see his success. Each died at age 94.

He credits his wife, the former Frances Stover of White County, as his loyal helpmate. The two of them met while working in a zipper plant in Cleveland, Ga., she as a machine operator and he as a mechanic. However, going from mechanic to a cook and restaurant owner didn't faze him one bit.

The Seabolts have one son, Mark, 21, newly graduated from the University of Georgia and now general manager of Hartwell's first steak house, Fletcher's. Their other children include a step-son, Ricky, who teaches in Augusta, and is recognized as a great bandleader; two step-daughters, Beverly and Gail of Anderson and Hartwell.

The year, 1996, has not been kind to Mr. Seabolt in a medical way, but he is rapidly on the mend. In February, he had a hiatal hernia removed, and three months later, underwent surgery for the removal of a benign brain tumor.

"After the latest surgery, I had five people come to see me at Emory the next day — four preachers and Billy Dilworth. I recognized Billy's voice, who was there, just a few hours after surgery."

Pressed about his decision to open the new restaurant, Mr. Seabolt answered, "When Mark graduated from Georgia, he wanted to come back to Hartwell, so we built Fletcher's, a million dollar plus investment, and it's the nicest restaurant in northeast Georgia. We can handle a volume of people — 194 in the main dining room, 154, 150, and 54 people in the other dining rooms."

Mr. Seabolt's pride and joy is meeting and talking to people of the county and area. They come in and say, "This is our restaurant."

Everything is handled by computer and Mr. Seabolt boasts there is no salad bar or hot bar, which he believes can be unsanitary with customers serving themselves.

There is a house specialty called "Fletcher's Rose," the answer to a "blooming onion," and its success sells dozens every day.

Despite his hectic schedule, which begins at 5 a.m. daily, Mr. Seabolt is close to a number of governmental leaders, and hosted a giant campaign fund-raiser for Gov. Zell Miller. He remembers when Mr. Miller confided on Spartanburg television that his favorite milkshake was butterscotch from the Dairy Queen, and he always said Towns County never had a D-Q.

Also, Mr. Seabolt pointed out that Max Cleland visited the other day, and the restaurant owner assisted in his campaign. Elbert Memorial Hospital's Tim Merritt and others took part in a wine-tasting seminar, and groups from all over have visited Fletcher's.

Mr. Seabolt takes pride in the fact that his Dairy Queen helped the Rev. Ted Kelley launch a successful holiday basketball tournament several years ago, and it will be repeated this year.

A big smile crossed his face when he remembered the big anniversary sale five years ago at the Hartwell Dairy Queen, when he repeated prices of 20 years earlier — with hamburgers, milkshakes, hot dogs or french fries going for a quarter. Mr. Seabolt tossed both hands in the air for emphasis and said, "There was a huge traffic jam to the middle of the square, and Police Chief Cecil Reno said it was the most traffic he had ever seen in Hartwell." The Seabolts unloaded 8,000 hamburgers and three bread trucks had to make special deliveries that day.

This 59-year-old legend says, "It's not right for a man to move into a town, take everything he can get out of it, and move on."

Fletcher and Frances Seabolt make up a dynamic duo, a phenomenon Hartwell has never seen before.

Bingo is a lot like life

Death is no respecter of persons or organizations.

It was evident the other night when we returned to American Legion Post 7 in Gainesville for a game of bingo.

The crowd was large, the enthusiasm of the sponsoring Legion members and their auxiliary continued to be contagious and inviting, but there was something missing.

People. And faces.

After checking with Ray Shubert, Post Commander for two straight years, we were to learn of the death in the past few months of people like Andy Rylee, 75, known as the "Apple Man." Mr. Rylee always sat at a back table, surrounded by small sacks of apples, which he sold to fellow players.

Mr. Rylee, we learned, died earlier this year of a heart attack, and his brother found him the next morning, after he succumbed during the night.

Ironically, Mr. Shubert said the good man, who never married, had won $750 in bingo games that week, and bingo had been his life.

Fortunately, Mr. Rylee didn't let the zaniness of the Georgia lottery capture his money, because he always told folks he knew where the money was going at the American Legion, and he wasn't sure just where all the funds were going for the lottery.

We aren't sure either, except for the point that the executive director is making $130,000 per year that we know of, more than the governor's salary, and who knows how many more are on the payroll of this private corporation.

Yet, good groups like the Legion, Elks, VFW or even the Catholic church can only give a maximum of $1,100 per night, while the Georgia lottery has untapped millions to give away, or to gather, and the lawmakers made that legal, and isn't that crazy?

But back to death.

The face of Mrs. Peggy Hayes, 60, was absent, and Mr. Shubert said she died only a couple of months ago, a victim of cancer.

"Peggy was one of the most graceful people, and she died with dignity, and worked up until two weeks prior to her death," said Mr. Shubert.

Her husband, Leonard, former tax assessor in Hall and White Counties, and past-post commander, was helping with the games the other night, and his teenage son was playing bingo across from Mr. and Mrs. Robert Cason of Cleveland, who also have a home in Red Hill and Franklin County.

The Hayes' had a daughter, and the family is carrying on as she would have wanted, but there's a void in the concession stand where she had a ready smile, and took orders for hotdogs, homemade cakes, coffee and Coca-Cola.

And then there was another missing place where Mrs. Rachel Kinsey sat for years on Tuesday and Wednesday nights. She died a few weeks ago at 73.

The death of Mr. Rylee now makes the total of three of the men who sat on the back row and played the game, which benefits the less fortunate in the Gainesville area.

The first to go was Ralph, the "Flower Man," about whom we wrote months ago, and the second was W. J. Porter of Homer, who ran a successful dance at Homer and Clarkesville before his sudden death. He was in his 70s.

"You'll never know how many people we have lost since we started up bingo in 1980," Mr. Shubert was saying. "My wife, Barbara, and I think a lot of times about how many are not with us anymore, but then we always think about how much happiness we must have brought to those who have gone on, and how much sunshine they created in the lives of humanity."

And then we thought, *bingo is a lot like life. You win some and you lose some.*

Then, like life, you must play to win, thank God, and those souls all across the country, who are using bingo markers and paper pads night after night, keeping their minds clear, and helping others along the way.

Carnesville abuzz over military wedding

Carnesville's first military wedding ever — and possibly Franklin County's first — took place the other Saturday night before a standing room only crowd of relatives and friends at Carnesville First United Methodist Church.

Miss Lee Sullivan became Mrs. Charles Hall in a beautiful ceremony, that lasted less than 45 minutes, in the same church the bride's father, Dennis Sullivan, attended as an MYF'er a half century ago in the same history-rich sanctuary.

The couple exchanged vows before God and mankind, after the bride's father and family gave her away in the traditional manner. Mr. Sullivan, a long-time registered pharmacist, surprised the bride with a kiss on the cheek.

The Rev. Gary McWhorter, a former pastor, officiated at the ceremony and, at the end, six new Army lieutenants from West Point and Harvard crossed swords, forming a canopy over the newlyweds as they exited the church, and one of the groom's friends, Lt. Clete Johnson, told the bride, "Mrs. Hall, welcome to the Army." Lt. Johnson is the son of former Congressman and Mrs. Don Johnson.

The bride and groom have distinguished themselves as honor graduates in both high school and college, and Lt. Hall is reporting for active duty in the next few weeks at Ft. Benning, Ga., then to El Paso, Tex. and on to Honolulu, Hawaii.

The bride's mother, Bobbie Sullivan, is also a registered pharmacist, and the groom is the son of Mr. and Mrs. Larry O. Hall of Lavonia.

The ceremony was one to be remembered for a long time, and the military touch took on an added dimension to the June exchanging of vows.

82

Who will take grandmother?

Anderson, S.C. auto executive, Ralph Bolt, must be an empathetic man. He passes along, by way of Roy Gaines of the TV station a poem written by "Grannie Bolt," his own grandmother, who composed it at the age of 86 in 1965. Read over our shoulder:

"Who will take Grandmother?
Who will it be?
All of us want her—I'm sure you'll agree.
Let's call a meeting. Let's gather the clan.
Let's get it settled as soon as we can.
I'm sure, in a big family, there's certainly one willing to give her
    a place in the sun."
"Strange how we thought she'd never wear out;
But see how she walks, it's arthritis—no doubt.
Her eyesight is faded; her memories are dim.
She's apt to insist on the silliest whim.
When people get older, they become such a care.
She must have a home, but the question is Where?"
"Remember the days when she used to be spry?
Baked her own cookies, and baked her own pies?
Helped us with lessons and mended our seams?
Kissed away troubles and minded our dreams?
Wonderful Grandmother, we all loved her so!
Isn't it dreadful—she's no place to go?"
"One little corner is all she would need;
A shoulder to cry on; her Bible to read;
A chair by the window with sun coming through;
Some pretty spring flowers still covered in dew.
Who'll warm her with love, so she won't mind the cold?
Oh, who will take Grandmother—Now that she's old?"
"What" Nobody wants her!
Oh, yes, there's one willing to give her a place in the sun—where she
    won't have to worry or wonder or doubt, and she won't be our
    problem to bother about.
Pretty soon now, God will give her a bed. But who'll dry our eyes—
    when dear Grandmother is dead?"

"Trigger" Thomason now has a seat on the 50-yard line

Arthur "Trigger" Thomason was an unusual man.

The tough soul you saw on the football field on Friday nights, first as a player, then as coach, a football official, and a spectator, was not the total "Trigger" Thomason.

The real Mr. Thomason, who left us not more than a week ago after a battle with his heart, had a razor-sharp mind that kept its scalpel strength until near end.

As an example, his devoted wife, Gaynelle Thomason, who has served as our secretary for almost a year, was debating about the name, "Christopher Reeve," and her husband quietly interjected that the name was not Reeves, but Reeve. He was that precise in sports. He was devoted to his family and friends, and he loved them all.

We remember interviewing him live on *Mountain Morning* about being a Pearl Harbor survivor in World War II, and talking about that ill-fated day for the Americans living on the island of Hawaii, where the Japanese struck on a Sunday morning, at a time when many of our soldiers were out partying, and how anything but war was on their minds, and his face lit up like a Christmas tree.

Mr. Thomason talked about all that and told of losing buddies in battle. One time, in a foxhole in the South Pacific, he said every soldier in that foxhole was killed except him.

Mr. Thomason did a lot of private contemplation in his 76 years, and he kept up with every facet of community, state and national life until the end.

That fateful Sunday afternoon on December 7, 1941, was to change Arthur "Trigger" Thomason's life forever — and life for all humanity.

A visit to the site today will bear that out. We salute him for his courage and dedication to education, and to the youth and the young-at-heart, and the fact remains his shoes will be difficult to fill.

Somehow, we get the feeling that Trigger will, for the first time in several years, have a 50-yard line seat between the hedges in Sanford Stadium, where his beloved Bulldogs romped and stomped so many times in the years that he was able to go and watch.

84

Graduates, the real struggle is beginning

Dear Grad:

This is an annual thing — a letter to you. We've written it 36 times.

This step you have taken, or are about to take, is one of the most important in life — other than a decision for the Good Lord, or for a mate or an occupation.

But the occasion is more than a symbol. It's more than moving the tassel of the cap from one side to the other.

It is much more than walking down the long aisle of a church, or auditorium, or gym or football field to the accompaniment of music, or sheer silence.

If you are graduating from high school, it marks the end of 12 long years of study and preparation.

If you are finishing college, it either means two, four, six, or eight years of additional study.

While your sacrifices may have been many, consider those made by your parents, grandparents, or others who helped show the way.

You'll forget some of your teachers. You don't think so now, but you will.

The good point to make is there are those things instilled that you'll never forget.

You'll laugh at those who said high school years are the best in life, but you won't be laughing a decade from now.

We would err if we told you life would be a bed of roses. There will be many thorns along the way, but such is life. The roses come with the thorns.

This is the year we elect a president, members of Congress, and officers on the local and state levels.

Your day is seeing the likeness of Newt Gingrich, who would cut Medicaid, reduce Medicare and Lord knows what else in the federal treasury; yet Mr. Gingrich and those of his ilk never turn down their big paychecks, complete with massive insurance perks and grandiose lifestyles.

Fortunately, you don't know anything about war. Only what you read or hear or see on TV or in rental movies.

Vietnam was hell, Korea was hell. World War II, the war supposed to end all wars, was a double hell, and there are some brave former soldiers in hospitals across the globe today, still suffering from battle scars.

Your day has seen the advent of television talk shows with a cast that includes names like Montel Williams, Geraldo, Rush Limbaugh, Oliver North and a guy named Neal Boortz on the Georgia level.

This cast seems to think they hold the world in their hands, but one of these days, they will be like the fertile fields of grain. They will be picked, gathered and even blown away in a breeze.

Your kind faces medical science, which can cure heart trouble with a triple bypass, but, somehow, still can't cure the common cold or a broken heart.

And don't forget. Some of your classmates will drink your booze this June and forget all about you six months from now. They will write in your annual, "Your friend forever," and many won't be able to recall your name by the year 2000. Instead, they will be in their glare of rose-colored glasses.

The good thing to say is there is a world of untapped knowledge out there and satellites still to be touched.

The sky is the limit if you will only apply yourself and continue to listen to wiser, older heads who used to think, like you, they had the solutions in their teens.

Remember, there are more good people than bad, and more sunny days than rainy days, and keep that in mind, with a lot of positive notes, as you walk down that aisle to graduate.

Godspeed and may the wind be at your back.

If only life could be simple

"Wonder why they took it off, Dilworth?" asked Doyle Williams the other day after hearing an audio from the old Lum and Abner radio show.

The question was more fact than fiction, and one radio and federal executives may have to answer for two preceding generations and generations still to be.

The Lum and Abner broadcast, a down-home 30-minute comedy aired on radio and later made into movies, struck at the heart of real America and the soul, where we got much of our real stuff when the going was rough in the 1940s.

In one episode, Lum and Abner, two hillbillies from Pine Ridge, Ark., and operators of the "Jot 'Em Down" store, depicted a trip to Washington, D.C., after being invited to the inauguration of Harry S. Truman. Characters in Pine Ridge donated a hen to carry to Mrs. Truman, and they had all sorts of trouble making it to the White House on Pennsylvania Avenue, where they were directed to the Blair House, where the Trumans were living while the biggest house in the country was undergoing repairs.

Lum swore he was going to give the chicken to the next person who came along, and Abner and a friend waited while Lum talked at length to a gentleman wearing glasses and a dark overcoat. When Lum returned, he told them the man said he would deliver the chicken immediately, and Abner noted that the man walked right through the front door at the Blair House so he must have known where he was going.

Lum said he told the man the chicken, which had already laid one egg on the trip, was a Rhode Island Red, and wondered if Mr. Truman could carry it.

"The man told me he carried it one time before and he was sure Mr. Truman could carry it again," said the likable Lum Edwards. This was just one of the many punch lines delivered in the comedy made only for radio, but perfectly tailored for the motion picture screen.

The other side of the audio was a ditty about Lum Edwards entering the insurance business and selling policies for three dollars a year. Some townspeople wondered if they could buy a dime's worth to last for a day. Suddenly, everybody in Pine Ridge was either sick from food poisoning or from home and auto accidents, and the Lum Edwards Insurance Company was soon absorbed by a takeover from some big city company up East.

How true and how honest!

This radio classic, which sold for about four bucks at the Cracker Barrel Restaurant in Anderson, S.C., turned out to be an hour of great fun for the wife, Joyce, and for all who would listen for the next few days.

Which brings us back to Doyle's basic questions of why.

Why can't life be simple anymore? Back in that era, nobody

ever heard of a stress test, and a nervous breakdown wasn't even in the dictionary.

The word Alzheimer's wasn't even in instruction manuals at Emory University or other big medical schools, and nobody knew much about anything that killed, except heart attacks and an all-encompassing ailment called consumption.

That was before the day of television and its gigantic hold on a nation. That was prior to the era of a lottery, where people fork over millions of dollars every month in a state where rural roads are being ignored, some of our state politicians have fat wallets comparable to baseball players, and the poor old people are mired down in gosh-awful nursing homes with diagnoses of Alzheimer's disease, ulcers, heart attacks or strokes, and the end result is a do-nothing generation and death.

Why can't life be simple like Lum and Abner?

Why can't life be simple like Amos and Andy?

Why can't life be simple like Henry Aldrich? And, incidentally, the main character, Henry Aldrich, spent a tour of duty at old Camp Toccoa on Currahee Mountain during World War II.

Simply put, why can't life be without verbal embroidery, and the semi-silliness and vulgarity abounding in virtually every hour of radio, television and the movies in this year?

Oh, oh, would to God life could get to be so plain, humble, down-to-earth, and good again!

Capt. Dudley: a mission

If there is anything Capt. C. C. Dudley can boast with pride, it's the fact that Tugaloo Home Health Agency, which he founded in 1978, is possibly the finest of its type in the nation.

"Nothing makes me more proud than to know we have made it possible for thousands of people to remain at home and receive competent medical care without going into a long-term nursing facility," declared the long-time military chief.

Captain Dudley, always on the move, was talking on his car telephone north of Charlotte the other day for this interview, and he was bound for Baltimore, Md., to meet with old Navy buddies and visit a ship, the *USS Turner*, which he commanded during his brilliant military career.

The northeast Georgia native son met his wife, Joyce McKenzie of England, while he was in the military, and they presently live in a beautiful home in Royston.

The Captain was in the Merchant Marines six years before entering the U. S. Navy, where he served with distinction for 28 years, and retired with the rank of captain in 1978.

He did not waste many miles before launching the Tugaloo Home Health Agency, first embracing eight counties in a venture that would take him into 13 counties by late 1996, with the main office in Lavonia and other offices in Clarkesville, Toccoa, Gainesville, and Clayton.

He is particularly proud that his employees now number a whopping 450, including registered nurses, licensed practical nurses, nursing assistants, and professionals in every specialty, including speech, occupational and physical therapy.

"I don't think I could be more proud of our staff and their devotion to the sick in northeast Georgia," he noted.

"Our people go as far north as Clayton, Forsyth, and Dawson Counties, and as far south as Elbert County," he added.

How does this amazing man unwind?

"I always keep busy and I find I do better when I stay busy all the time," he confessed.

The Captain has just been re-elected for a third term to the Georgia Federation and Military Retiree Coalition, which numbers over 130,000 members in all 159 counties in Georgia.

As executive director of Tugaloo Home Health Agency, Captain Calvin C. Dudley is a man who knows the seas and the land — and the people who occupy both spaces.

On column writing in 1989

The fellow or woman who pounds out a column doesn't exactly enjoy the *Life of Riley* in the process.

Instead, he lives in, more or less, a pressure cooker and wonders what might be around the next corner or minute for a column.

Sometimes, possible topics are a dime a dozen and ideas crop up from everywhere and everyone. Other times, there are complete blanks.

A long-time friend in this business, Paul Hemphill, who has filled in for us several times, believes a columnist hits on topics of interest for the general public two days out of seven.

And Hemphill, with whom we shared a desk at the old *Atlanta Times*, used to sit in near-anguish working on a column.

"If I could just get the first paragraph, and the last, I'd have it made," he said.

Slowly, Hemphill moved his frail fingers through a full head of hair and walked to the wire machines three or four times in the course of composing a daily piece.

When thoughts became slow for the talented man, he would walk one block down the street to the Tower Restaurant and sit with the boys in the back.

"Sometimes, it gives me ideas for a column," he said. "Often, it gives a chance to find out what they are thinking."

There were days Hemphill would drift into the newsroom at midnight and dash off a column in a half hour.

"I was almost asleep when this item hit me, and I got up and came down here while it was fresh," he said.

We knew his feelings. Well.

Often, at 3 o'clock in the morning when the radio isn't tuned to WSM in Nashville, an idea comes to mind, but is forgotten by dawn.

For a time, we licked that with a pencil and pad by the side of the bed.

Writing a column means following the gamut of life.

We learned long ago it is best to keep the public guessing what might be next and erase the fear of being cast into a firm mold.

A preacher-friend, who employed the same psychology, consistently kept his congregation wondering what might happen next.

One Sunday, he dispensed with the announcements and used only one opening song, then went into a 19-minute sermon.

The next Sunday night, he had three congregational hymns, preached two minutes, and said the benediction.

Which bowled over some of the old heads in the church, but they came back the next Sunday.

Only trouble is, brevity wouldn't work in column writing.

A two-minute sermon would be like saying "hello" and "good-bye."

Which might not be bad some days.

There are more stars glittering in the sky

"Looks like I'm always calling with bad news," said Harold Corn from his home in Commerce the other Saturday night.

Then in sort of a rambling tone of voice that showed hurt and loss, he relayed news about the death just hours before of his 79-year-old mom, Mrs. John Corn.

The voice on the end of the line picked up momentum a little and continued, "Mama got sick at home and we rushed her to the hospital in Royston, and she died about midnight. She said her heart was hurting awfully bad."

Mr. Corn then broke down a few times and said he was holding up as best he could.

The only son of Mr. and Mrs. John Corn, this 56-year-old man had been a lifelong friend to the Dilworth family, and his father was a friend to our father when cotton was king and work was the only thing they knew to do.

A month before, Mr. Corn called and told about the illness of his granddaughter, and said she was diagnosed with the same heart problem that caused the death of Mr. Corn's wife, Jeanette, in her late 30s.

We advised him to seek two or three medical opinions, and he and his son, Tony, did just that, and found a lady doctor in

New York who said she could control the problem with medication.

Mr. Corn and his second wife, Betty, whom he met years ago, joined Tony and his family on an auto trip to the doctor, and Mr. Corn became ill with pancreatitis.

Elton Collins, the Commerce banker, relayed the message of Mr. Corn's hospitalization in a New Jersey hospital, and we placed a call and talked about a half hour.

"I'm awfully weak, but I'm better, and they say I can take the plane home in a couple of days," he said.

Four nights after he called us of his mother's death, three calls were placed to our answering machine in Cornelia, and all conveyed the same sad message — "Harold Corn died tonight at Athens Regional Medical Center and we thought you would want to know."

In a way, it was a shocker, and in another way, it wasn't.

Mr. Corn's longtime pharmacist friend, Dennis Sullivan of Carnesville, had wondered aloud with us whether or not this good man's heart would take him through his mother's funeral.

He seemed to bear up well in the Ginn Funeral Home chapel, where singers known to his mother sang three gospel songs, and two ministers spoke good words about the grand little lady who used to sell quilts and cloth.

Mr. Corn came from good stock. His father was an early diabetic, like the son, and he and Mrs. Corn would drop by the radio station in Toccoa, and the father would rush into the studio with two simple requests. He wanted to hear "Walk Through This World With Me" by George Jones and "Could I Talk You Into Loving Me Again" by Wynn Stewart.

Harold Corn was more than brave. He was more than courageous. If there is a word stronger than tough, that would apply to this individual.

Consider the fact he cared for Jeanette, who literally died in his arms and then took in his father-in-law, Ben Brewer of Red Hill, in the early stages of prostatic cancer, and watched him perish away in the home he and Jeanette shared for years.

When Donnie Craft of Hartwell introduced Harold to Betty, that would change his life, and Betty gave him 13 good years of life at their beautiful home on Dogwood Trail in Commerce, where we occupied a basement apartment for five years, and got to know Harold like a brother.

Betty's life had not been easy either. She lost her husband to cancer, and a pretty 18-year-old daughter, who died running track near their Commerce home.

Harold's tough luck began anew four years ago when an elderly couple from Florida pulled up in two cars at his service station on Interstate 85, and the lady asked him to pump gas for both cars. Mr. Corn agreed, although this would change his life forever.

He stood at the back of one car pumping gas, and the lady pressed the accelerator in the second car, and caught Mr. Corn at the knees, and he was knocked to the ground.

Within 12 hours, he had lost one leg, many pints of blood, but kept his spirit.

And, after hours of open heart surgery at Emory Hospital, Mr. Corn bounced back and continued to operate his station, recognized several times as a Texaco Station of the Year.

The mind is threaded with the question, "Why do bad things happen to good people?" and we always revert to that exalting sermon by Dr. Roy O. McClain, who told of asking God why his own mother was dying from cancer that started on an ear.

At the end of his sermon, Dr. McClain gave the answer, "And the dumb stars glittered."

And two funerals later, of a mother and her son, in 1995, we say with all honestly that there are more stars in the sky than three weeks ago.

Homer: world's biggest hunt

Give or take on a Saturday night, the population of Homer, Ga. is no more than 600.

But, on Easter Sunday afternoons, the town boasts more people per square foot than New York City, or Hong Kong.

The reason: The world's largest Easter egg hunt.

The ritual, and you can call it that, started in 1959 — 30 years ago— when O. S. Garrison, a man 50 years ahead of his time, launched a public egg hunt for kids of Homer.

After the patriarch's death, the hunt has gotten larger each year, thanks to Mrs. Lillie Garrison, widow of O. S., and their two sons, Buster and Herbert, their wives, Syble and Betty, and families.

A few tourist attractions and shopping malls tried to compete and call theirs the world's largest, but they didn't attain first-base status.

At the age of 12 just five years ago, young Oscar Garrison, son of Herbert and Betty, armed himself with newspaper clippings of the preceding 25 years and put them in the hands of *Guiness Book of World Records*.

Each year thereafter, Guiness book lists the Garrison egg hunt as "the world's largest."

Former Georgia Transportation Chief Tom Moreland gave the signal to put up city limits signs noting the title, and passers-by can see them throughout the year.

This year's hunt, planned Easter Sunday afternoon exactly at 2 o'clock, will feature 72,000 hen eggs hidden in the grassy pastureland of both brothers. And, for good measure, there will be 60,000 candy eggs and several prize eggs.

Lt. Gov. Zell Miller and his wife, Shirley, will be there. Former Gov. Lester Maddox and his wife, Virginia, will attend. Congressman and Mrs. Ed Jenkins will also be there. The Garrisons expect a bumper crop of politicians, and all are welcomed, they said. Elliott Caudell and Richard Acree of Toccoa are perennial attendees.

"We're sweating out the weather right now," Herbert Garrison was saying the other day. "Easter is early this year, and the weather can play tricks, but we've never, ever been rained out in 30 years."

Like the World's Fair, the egg hunt gets larger each year.

The Garrison clan can count on a large number of Northeast Georgia and Western South Carolina people, plus a bumper crop of visitors who are in the area for the day.

The unique event has drawn attention of residents of Hawaii the past three years.

"Each Easter Sunday, a radio announcer in Honolulu calls me and puts me on the air live, and I tell the people about the world's largest egg hunt in Homer, Ga.," Garrison explains. "They really can't believe it, but they heard about in the Guiness Book."

The brothers say the feat would be impossible without the help of friends and neighbors, who get up before dawn Easter

94

Sunday and build fires under wash pots and prepare the fresh eggs for boiling.

Homer, Ga. is indeed on the world map one time a year, and no other town can make that statement!

Now, the road turns again

Editor's note: This is Billy's final column from the *Athens Daily News* where he wrote from 1972 until 1987.

Every day, there are changes in the road of life.

A major transition came for us in newspapering in 1964 when a move was made from Anderson, S.C., to the *Atlanta Times*. A daring mission, if you please, of serving as daily column writer and state editor for a new, fledging statewide paper.

Publisher James C. Davis, a grand guy, a loyal Republican who knew Congress, but unfortunately could not fathom newspapering, and the paper died 10 months later.

They designated us to write the final column on page 1-B. It was titled, "The road ends."

We noted that a few corpuscles died saying goodbye to the Atlanta area and people across Georgia. At one point, *The Times* attained a circulation of 110,000.

We left numerous friendships that day in Atlanta and Luther Thigpen, managing editor, had assembled some of the most competent news people from throughout the South.

The last time we saw them was the moment we all autographed the final edition, wept into handkerchiefs unashamed, and walked out the door at 700 Forest Road.

We have never forgiven Atlanta city fathers for renaming that stretch of road Ralph McGill Boulevard because it was the opposite of the McGill liberal stance that the conservative paper was built.

Today, the road turns again.

After writing a daily column until a few months ago, for the *Athens Daily News* most years since 1965 and writing longer than any other person in modern times, it is difficult, like in Atlanta, to sit at a typewriter and compose another final column.

An Elbert County native, the Rev. H. Dan Rice, pastored the rural Allens Methodist Church in Red Hill, where we grew up, picked cotton and walked to school and tugged at girl's pig-tails, stood on the wooden front porch at the home place one day in 1953, "Don't let 'em change your style at the university, Billy," he said. He put his hand on the shoulder of a thin, gangly farm lad.

That stuck through the years, and we've tried to maintain our identity.

One of the finest newspaper publishers in the South, the late Wilton E. Hall, who came up from the middles of a cotton patch in Starr, S.C., told his reporters in the mid-1950s, "You're not writing for people with a college degree on our paper. You're writing for a person with an average of an eighth-grade education."

That rings through our mind constantly.

It hasn't been easy writing upwards of two decades for a university town, where professors abound in every field with doctorates and super-doctorates.

But it has been a challenge knowing they were out there — probably grinning under their breath at times on a simple stance taken by a country boy involving topics from possums and Paul Silas of Young Harris to the Eisenhower, Johnson, Nixon, Ford, Carter, and Reagan occupancy of the grandest house of all in Washington.

But those professors endured — and we are grateful. Many inspired us with little notes. Some were typed. Others were penciled on paper and sent to Lavonia.

We've enjoyed setting another record in Northeast Georgia journalism — interviewing thousands of people in the "On The Road" series that ran sometimes as often as seven days a week in the *Athens Daily News.*

We had some of the finest photographers in the land to ride with us on dirt roads and city streets to locate the people who make up this great part of Northeast Georgia. We tried to convey that the ditch diggers and the pole climbers are just as important as the jet set and country club crowd.

We are grateful to the employers who endured all this time.

The roles and leadership of publishers Bill Bailes, Buddy

Hayden, Bob Chambers and Mark Smith will always be imprinted in our memory bank.

The kind leadership exhibited by Hank Johnson, executive editor, is very much appreciated too. We watched Hank cover his first story — a car wreck a few miles from One/Press Place — on a sunny afternoon in the summertime.

And, now the road takes another turn. New challenges await and we are saying goodbye here today.

Maybe the best way to do that is to remember a couple or three points the late Dr. Roy O. McClain, one of the nation's top five ministers, made to this country product, either in sermon from Atlanta First Baptist Church or many times spent talking.

• Of humankind, McClain said "A man ought not ever forget where he was, where he is, or where he's going."

• Of the most noble mission of all, going to Heaven, McClain said, "No one will ever get to Heaven — until Heaven first gets into them."

• Of the last time any mortal soul had contact with Dad, dying at age 77 in a ground-floor room at Hart County Hospital in 1975, McClain grabbed the once-strong right hand and said, "Mr. Dilworth, if you know who I am, squeeze my hand two times." Dad squeezed tightly four times.

"Well, I told you last time to eat all the blackeyed peas, cornbread, and drink all the buttermilk you could," McClain said softly. "Now I'm saying you don't have to fight anymore. Just relax and hold my hand and I want you to go to sleep. I'll be right here with you."

Dad was asleep in five minutes, did not have a moment's pain, and death came just before dawn.

Thank God!

And, farewell, loyal reader!

'I wish Henry was here'

Doyle Williams, the mountain man from Baldwin, summed up the biggest birthday party he's ever had by saying, off camera, "I wish Henry Dillard was alive and could be here."

The comment came in the midst of a few teardrops from Doyle, everybody's friend from the hill-country, honored on live television Saturday night from WNEG-TV at Toccoa on his 60th birthday anniversary.

He even dressed up for the occasion, abandoning his overalls and long-tailed shirt for Sunday trousers, dress shirt, and tie. He still wore his two hats for Community Bank and Habersham Bank in separate phases of the show. Among Doyle's trademarks are his hats and dancing.

He danced for the camera Friday night at the J&J Center.

Jerry Farmer brought Doyle a pocket knife and a quarter. Harold and Betty Corn of Commerce gave him a fancy shirt from Taylor's; the TV staff presented him with a huge cake baked by Toccoa Bakery; Brenda Thomas of Habersham brought him another cake from Gainesville; and Bill Raper, Verlin Reece and James Miller of Tri -County Quality Foods of Commerce delivered a third big cake, baked by Seagraves Sweet Shop at Commerce.

The three grocers also brought three bags of Vidalia onions, cartons of Cokes, potato chips, and paper plates.

Two women from Cornelia came down in clown costumes and kissed "Professor" Doyle on both cheeks and he had lipstick smears. Bill and Gail Raper's 11-year-old daughter, Julie, hugged Doyle right in front of the TV cameras.

Dr. Max Kent, the orthopedic surgeon from Anderson, S.C., and the TV show's "resident physician," gave Doyle two colorful cards and a $20 bill. He also read the Memorial Day weather forecast before he returned to South Carolina.

Five people vying for a $25 first-place prize called into the show to sing "Happy Birthday." The winner, chosen by Brenda Thomas and John Defoor, camera people, was Mrs. Cliff Miller of Toccoa. Runners-up were Jim Ensley, manager of the Holiday Inn at Clemson, S.C.; Mrs. Nora Richard, an 86-year-old lady at 418 Audubon Place, Toccoa; Daniel Gainius of Toccoa; and Dale Lee of Route 3, Walhalla, S.C. Each received a $5 bill.

Someone jokingly told Doyle more money was spent singing "Happy Birthday" than his mama and daddy had to spend when he was born six decades ago somewhere around Habersham County.

Doyle grinned broadly.

A couple of viewers from Habersham County, Eddy and Betty LaPrade, presented him with a ceiling fan for his den — installed.

A cousin, Lessie York, from Marshall, Tex., called in to the show to wish him a happy birthday. He hadn't heard from her in 25 years.

And now, Doyle Williams is entering his seventh decade of living.

He has outlived his buddy, Henry Dillard, by one year and it is easy to see why he whispered, "I wish Henry could be here."

Didn't we all!

We told Dennis Sullivan, Carnesville pharmacist, one time long ago that we were losing friends in the wholesale numbers. And we'll never forget Mr. Sullivan's reply, "And those are the kind we can't replace, but I guess we should be making younger friends." The good man is right, and we'd better get to work, because it's going to take a bunch of the young ones to compensate for those rapidly leaving us here on earth.

The good point to make is that all of those we lose are in a much better place, where there is no pain, no time clocks, no fax machines, no cellular telephones and no worries.

She lost her 'will to live'

If doctors would open up and be honest, they would say the will to live is half the battle.

People are buried in every major city across the world every day because of the loss of the will to live.

It's happening today in Macon.

A month ago, they buried John Collins in a cemetery not far from the heart of this mid-Georgia city.

The man, in his early 80s, and his wife, the former Lala Bishop, had been the only survivors in a grinding two-car crash that left two occupants of the other car instantly dead.

The two in the first car were retired military ladies.

Collins lived little more than a week; complications set in and he died.

Mrs. Collins was able to return home with her injuries, but required the presence of the two daughters, Mrs. Bill Chandler of Commerce and Mrs. Bo Steele of Macon, almost constantly.

At one point, Mrs. Collins was alert and even told a son-in-law, Bill Chandler, the man from the funeral home was at the door to bring chairs for friends and a large coffee pot.

She was able to attend her husband's funeral, but returned home and to bed.

Two weeks ago, she told the daughters she wouldn't make it.

"I don't even know how to die," she said.

In the process, the sweet, kind 89-year-old Macon lady lost her desire to live. She looked over at the empty bed in the house here and wept a thousand times to herself.

That,and the injuries of the wreck, took its toll on the woman.

Just after 9 o'clock Wednesday night, Mrs. Collins died at the family residence. She had been in a coma for days.

And, this afternoon, they will have her funeral and burial in the same cemetery.

The daughters have pictures of a merry 1985 Christmas. Collins had his arms around his wife.

Mrs. Collins simply lost her will to live.

Now, they are together again. This time, forever.

Life is but a vapor and death is permanent.

And if mankind could distinguish between the difference while there is still time. . . .

'Almost persuaded...
now to believe'

"Almost persuaded, now to believe.
Almost persuaded, Christ to receive...
Seems now some soul to say,
Go spirit, go thy way.
Some more convenient day, on Thee I'll call"

The crowd of more than 100 worshippers sang that old hymn with feeling Sunday night at Fair Oaks United Methodist Church in Smyrna.

And two pastors long associated with Methodism in Northeast Georgia led the way in the 55-minute service, the first of a three-day revival at the growing church in Cobb County.

The Rev. E. J. McDonald, pastor, and his wife, Elizabeth, are in their fourth year of service to the church, but both were remembering other good years in the pastorate —— 1959–1963 —— on the Athens Circuit.

"I have a lot of good memories on the Athens Circuit," Mr. McDonald told us at a fellowship meal prior to the service.

The Augusta native introduced an Elbert County native, the Rev. Jack Gillespie, pastor of Skyland Methodist Church in Atlanta, guest speaker for the mini-revival, who keyed his opening sermon to the love of Jesus Christ and how He died on the cross almost 2,000 years ago.

"I believe Jesus Christ is just as much alive today as He can be," Mr. Gillespie told his Sunday night listeners. "Every now and then, my wife, Mary, and I go to the cemetery in Elberton where we have 12 relatives buried, but they're not there. They're with God in Heaven."

Earlier in the day, the preacher who once pastored Carnesville-Allens-Fairview Churches in Franklin County, told his members at Skyland to compare the big crowds on Palm Sunday many years ago to the crowd alone on Good Friday, the day Jesus was nailed to the cross.

"Picture that contrast and has it changed much today?" he asked.

A little 89-year-old lady, whose mind is as sharp as a 21-year-old, sat on the front row and listened intently.

A former Peace Corps worker, she had recited her love for the church just before opening hymn.

At the end of the service, they went up to the altar, one by one, then two by two, where they knelt as the organist played softly, "Almost Persuaded."

It was a different, but good, Sunday night.

Whatever happened to visiting?

We'd like to know:

• Why people don't "visit" any more. It's an art as lost as "borrowing" back on the farm.

• Why Washington politicians are still skillful at preparing diplomatic statements which usually have three sides and say nothing.

• What the major news stories will be five years from now.

• What the major news stories will be 10 years from now.

• How many general merchandise stores are around today — and what the number will be like in the year 2000.

• How many youngsters say "yes, ma'am" and "yes, sir" to their elders these days.

• Why our day seems more intent on baseball replays and instant breakfast than long-term care for friends and neighbors and relatives.

• How many souls remember when school lunches were free.

• How many adults recall when children carried box lunches to one-room schools.

• And how many remember when youngsters used to work after school.

• Whatever happened to "dunce caps."

• Why some preachers still think long sermons, and typically the kind they read, can hold a congregation's attention.

• What a computerized office will look like in five years.

• Why three or four offices utilizing computers have as much down time as operative time.

Easter: a day in finest hour

Easter Sunday should be the best day of the year.

This is the day that marks life's victory over death, a fact supported by the resurrection of Jesus almost 2000 years ago.

This is the season of the year when Spring bursts forth with the rebirth of trees and shrubs and plants.

In the days when farming was king in Northeast Georgia, farmers counted on Spring to mark the beginning of placing cotton and corn seed into the earth and of waiting for the dividends.

Easter Sunday is that one day of the year when people who don't darken the doors of church, except at Christmas, make their presence known.

The good part about that is Christmas and Easter give us hope for tomorrow.

And, Lord knows, we need all the tomorrows we can get because they make up yesterdays and a combination of tomorrows, todays, and yesterdays create the memory banks for humanity.

If the weatherman was right, today dawned bright and clear from Lincolnton to the south and Rabun Gap and Hiawassee and Gainesville to the north.

And the sunshine should heap tons of Heaven's rays below.

Some churches got an early start with sunrise services; others plan service at 11 a.m. and even later.

The world's largest egg hunt is planned at 2:30 p.m. today at Homer on the lawns of Herbert and Buster Garrison and the hunt is a living memorial to their dad, the late Oscar Garrison, a man a half century ahead of his time.

Easter Sunday should be the best day of the year. Enjoy!

A doctor reflects on a preacher

(Editor's Note — The Carnesville-Allens-Fairview Methodist churches lost their minister, the Rev. H. Frank Driskell, in an airplane crash — only shortly after his arrival at the pastorate. Dr. Robert Sullivan, the town's physician and a native of Carnesville, wrote his thoughts on the minister and his good works in a few short years.)

• • •

We have just come through the Frank Driskell interval in Carnesville, Ga. It was only a few days. It ended so abruptly, so unexpectedly.

Carnesville-Allens-Fairview charge of the United Methodist Church had just been sent a bright young pastor with promises of, "you're gonna like this guy." We were astir with his ministry, his visitations, his choir work, his educational programs. The whole congregation seemed excited. He was going to help us "understand the Methodist Church." Then suddenly he is no longer with us.

A shock wave of mourning has gone through the community carrying a strange awareness of just how expendable you can be. People are puzzled about their religion and the "acts of God." We are groping to find consolation.

Indeed, his life was consumed while ministering to us. He deserves to be on the history books of the Carnesville Methodist Church. An urgency to record a picture befitting the man is felt. How did he come to make such an impression in such a short period of time?

Right away you saw he was different, and he didn't care who knew it. He arrived in town with a beautiful family, horses, a pick-up truck, and a motorcycle. There was a flare of Americana-Georgia flavor.

Analyzing Frank D. wasn't difficult. He was a simple straight-forward man who had his decisions made and his lights turned on. The first thing he did in church was to introduce his family. Then he kept you spellbound with a sermon that lasted about 20 minutes. When he finished, you thought he had just started.

It didn't take anytime to see that Frank D. was a family man, an outdoorsman, and an "action" man. He had a moustache and walked with a springy step.

We were in the midst of a terrible drought. One of the very first functions was to put a message on the bulletin board out front — "Pray For Rain." We had rain. Then the bulletin board said "There Shall Be Showers — Praise The Lord."

He was nice to folks. You were struck with how friendly he was. Frank just flashed a big smile and made instant friends. After talking to him five minutes, you felt like you had known him forever.

A man of action, Frank didn't believe any progress could be made standing still, or spinning wheels. When thinking of Frank, the words of the poet kept ringing back "Let us then be up and doing, life is not a bitter stream."

He radiated a positive attitude. He imparted that keeping faith, believing in yourself, and maintaining confidence is what gets you by in this world. To live life to the fullest, and to live it with love. To keep a sense of pride without being too proud.

Frank was almost an outdoorsman, a maverick of sorts. He seemed almost untamed. He loved the natural. He loved to get up early and see the sun rise. He loved beaver trapping and the creatures of the wild. They seemed to invigorate him. There was always a new adventure in the outdoors.

Frank told that he had once been called a "reactionary." This happened because of some demonstrations about a certain political principle he felt needed changing. He later found out that another approach would be more effective. Nevertheless, reactionary spirit was in his blood.

Actually "cooperative" was a better way to describe Frank D. When he was hospitalized a couple days for an infection, a more cooperative patient could not be found. He approached the problem with "whatever needed to be done must be done." If it is done together, there is no problem.

Humility was undoubtedly one of his greatest qualities. At times he was so humble it would make you want to cry. There was no place for arrogance in this man. He stood six-foot-four, but you never got the feeling that he was looking down on you. He was low-key, and really stayed in the background unless he was in the pulpit.

Frank D. was a very happy person. He was satisfied and sure of what he was doing. There was so much happiness to be shared, and those who do not have it must be shown the way.

Yes, it was very easy to be envious of Frank D. with his youth, good looks and energy. He had the ability to really get the message across. People had already remarked "We won't have him long; he is going fast." Some members had become greedy, telling other churches "look what we've got." Then all of the sudden he is devoured by the elements on his way home from a pastor's school.

Like so many other missions which had tragic endings — the Challenger, for example.

One of the last memories of Frank D. was as he was leaving in a thunderstorm one night, he smiled big, pointed to a big wooden mallet in the back of his truck and said, "Hey, you see that!" Then he drove off in the rain.

Who was Frank Driskell? He was a Methodist minister of the Gospel of Jesus Christ, 1986 style. He was a "role-model Christian." He just touched down here on his race through life. He only got to preach at Carnesville four times. Some games only last four quarters. If you got his message about the game of life, then he scored a touchdown for you.

Carnesville-Allens-Fairview charge had a unique experience. We mourn, but should not grieve. We should rejoice that at one time we got to know Frank Driskell. He was our minister when he died, but he left us with enough spirit that we can surely say "Let us go on from this place..."

Can you name two happy souls?

The friend, with just a tad of gray showing in his full head of hair, stoked his pipe and responded to a question.

The question: "Can you name two happy souls?"

He puffed a time or two and brought forth an answer which could not be duplicated by a professor with a super-doctorate in philosophy.

"I don't know that I can," he said. "Because the whole world is living too fast."

The friend suggested he would like to go back to the day of the horse and buggy and kerosene lamps and cotton farming with plenty of work to be done by day and leisure time at night with family and friends.

"Back then, friends were friends and neighbors helped neighbors. If a family got sick, another family would pitch in and help — even if it meant plowing the crops and doing the chopping and hoeing and everything."

But back to the happy people bit.

The friend reasoned that today's zip-coded, jet-paced, much-ado-about-nothing world has caused us to become more interested in passing the Jones' on the curve than helping them around the curve.

That pretty much sizes it up.

We put the same question of naming two thoroughly-happy souls to a couple of people in their late 20s and early 30s last week, and they couldn't name two. Any two.

There was a time when a minister's name, and that of his wife, could be compiled in that list, but problems of the church are so multiplied today that they occupy much of the minister's time.

Oh, there are some who say they have been married 60 years without the first argument, but how much truth can we put in any of that?

Here in 1980, when we're seeking to discover two happy people, think of the multi-thousands presently being treated for mental illness, either through tranquilizers or other chemicals, and know full-well that this discovery is about like trying to find the proverbial needle in the haystack.

We might as well cheer up, however. Things aren't going to get a whole lot better, with gasoline prices almost escalating by the month and human beings' mania-for-more.

But to end on a positive note. All of us could do better if we would slow our speed, enjoy the sunrise and sunset, and try to be a friend to humanity.

Part II: two happy souls

Sunday's column, "Can You Name Two Happy Souls?" caused a stir in Sunday school classrooms and in the newsroom of *The Daily News* and the *Athens Banner-Herald*.

In that plot of type, we quoted a friend with a tad of gray in a full head of hair as saying he believed the fast pace of life in 1980 has almost caused an era of unhappiness.

The friend was answering a direct question of, "Can you name two happy people?"

Mrs. Meg McGriff, a talented editor of the *Athens Banner-Herald*, put the column on the bulletin board or some yon place and inscribed a note: "If you are a happy person, let's let ole Billy know."

There were 13 names, beginning with Meg, and including Hank Johnson, Brandy Grimes, Elaine Hayden, Conoly Hester, Jesse Jenkins, Richard D. Fowlkes, Emory Lavendar, Karen Jowers plus one, Mary Dell Borneman, Curt Zimmerman and the famous Hap Hazzard of sports.

The 13th slot belonged to 107-38-5145, age 33, 30601, whatever or whoever that may be.

Daily News copy editor Linda Jennings said she intended to sign the list, but a letter of intent is good only in sports or politics.

Obviously, there were many names associated with the papers absent from the list.

We wonder why.

And we truly hope all 13, including the one with the social security number, are genuinely happy.

If they aren't, they may be employing good psychology because more than half the battle is in the mind anyway.

And the mind still controls the body, they say.

If thinking snow produces snow, then thinking happiness ought to produce a little contentment.

Anyway, thanks, Meg. We needed that.

Next time someone asks us to point out truly happy people, we'll give directions to One/Press Place!

'With this ring I thee wed'

Here, in this picturesque mountain town of Helen, once a sleepy village but transformed into an Alpine showplace, the store-keepers sell trinkets and blankets and ice cream to tourists.

The spot, with a population of 250 normally, but as much as 10,000 on weekends in the summer, is abuzz with hometowner and visitor taking in the mountain air, hearing the Chattahoochee River roll toward the ocean and parts unknown.

Thursday was no exception.

There were cars from Florida, Louisiana, Ohio, Michigan, Oregon and counties like Habersham, Stephens, Clarke, Hall, DeKalb, Fulton and, of course, home base in White.

Shop owners say they see it all.

Ross Cloer, on duty as a registered pharmacist at Pittman's Pharmacy said he is constantly amazed at the steady stream of tourists.

"I can tell a tourist at first glance," Cloer was saying. "You can't help but notice."

He sees honeymooners all the time.

"Sometimes, their cars are plastered with 'just married' and that's a dead give-away," he grinned.

Thursday morning, in a local shop where they sell cheese and rings in the same location, an elderly man who might be described as "The Bard of Helen" took his guitar in hand and addressed a couple in their mid-20s from Florida.

"Oh, just married, I see," he said. "I will sing a Christian song for you."

He asked their first names and immediately went into a song for Helen and Jimmy.

A dozen tourists looked on sheepishly.

"I guess it's my sixth sense which tells me about newlyweds," he said. "And, because of your occasion, I'm giving you one of my Christian albums. It won't cost you a dime.

Quickly, a little lady who will never see 75 again walked up to the couple, and said, "I hope married life brings you the best."

They cooed and thanked her.

"Weddings are so romantic," she went on. "I'll never forget my own vows, particularly, "With this ring I thee wed."

The man put down his guitar.

The ring business wasn't much on the rainy day, but his old-timey hoop cheese was going well.

'Going back' proves quite painful

Shuffling through old papers and bygone files can be as depressing as a death in the family.

Lately, we've had occasion to do some housecleaning at Red Hill and this involved the transition of papers from their long-term stay on shelves to a box called "discard."

It has been a painful experience.

Cousins Fred and Ruby and Bobby Davis and Mozelle Suggs of Greenville, S.C., and Kathryn Pickren of Lavonia helped with the experience and it was mind-shattering.

Dad died in 1975 after a lingering illness and Mom, who died in 1984, had saved more than 700 sympathy cards and messages of condolence.

There was a typed letter from former President Carter saying he had tried to call and couldn't get through.

A two-page letter from a longtime friend at Commerce conveyed the message that "this hour shall pass, although it will seem slow."

There were numerous handwritten messages of sympathy, including one who simply said, "I care."

Mom had wanted to discard much of the old correspondence, but the son insisted much of the stuff be retained.

Sorting through old papers can be about as depressing as anything.

Mom had saved many obituaries from newspapers in the 1940s and 1950s. There was one containing the death of her father, W.I. Davis, and her mother, Mrs. Josie Holbrook Davis.

If she were here today, she would want those kept and they were not discarded.

Instead, Fred and Ruby Davis carried a big batch of yellow clippings to their Greenville home. They also had other paraphernalia.

Mom was a stickler for saving quilts, the old-fashioned kind that women spent many hours making over a quilting frame or perhaps at a quilting bee. Kathryn Pickren carried a couple home with her, and they are being retained too.

There was the silver shovel given by General Telephone to the news media when Lavonia switched on to its computer terminal several years ago. It is being saved.

Mom kept elaborate scrapbooks and there was a faded photo of her and Dad about the time they married. It is a prized possession.

Somewhere, there is a copy of the Carnesville Methodist Messenger, printed by the late Rev. W. A. Purcell. It contained the marriage of B.Q. and Pearl Davis Dilworth in the parsonage at Carnesville. It will be kept too.

There is the taped funeral for Dad in 1975 with officiating ministers — the late Dr. Roy O. McClain, the Rev. Cecil Dudley and the Rev. Jack Gillespie — and they sound as clear as though they are speaking through the sound system today.

And there is the taped funeral of Mom back in 1984.

One dresser drawer contained a picture of Bulga, a Boston terrier that lived to be 12 years old and used to love to ride in the trailer back of the John Deere tractor. Bulga spent half his time in Hunter's Creek getting wet while the people with whom he lived chopped cotton and corn down on the Pulliam Place.

They say mankind can never "go back" home.

"Going back" through old files and papers and memorabilia can be depressing indeed!

'A wound time can't erase'

"Tell me, dear, are you satisfied
to be footloose and fancy-free....
you've left
A Wound Time Can't Erase."

It was your typical Sunday afternoon crowd at a downtown restaurant. Half the customers were locals from church and the other half came from Florida and tourist spots unknown.

They were doing a booming business selling steaks and seafood platters while pretty waitresses skirted about, making sure of the coffee and tea refills.

A guy who apparently owns the restaurant had a T-Model car parked out front and he walked through the front door and sat down at the front booth. He was wearing a hat typical of the 1890s and he seemed to be having the time of his life.

Small talk was as plentiful from diners. It always is—not only in Franklin, N.C., but any town any Sunday.

Somehow, conversation seems more informal on Sunday afternoons than other days.

Music wafted through the big dining room and one quick listen revealed it was Floyd Cramer at the piano.

As we entered, Floyd, really a bashful fellow in person and in recording sessions in Nashville, was playing "Last Date," the monster record in the early 1960s.

A pretty young thing in a table next to ours made some mention of "that song surely is pretty. What's the name of that?" A lady twice her age, obviously her mother, quickly answered "Last Date. It came out about the year you were born."

The blue-eyed honey twinkled her eyes and seemed impressed with the music.

It was later into the Floyd Cramer album that he played a tune which struck a responsive chord.

The piano was belting out notes of the song made popular two decades ago by Stonewall Jackson of Moultrie, Ga.

The words went like this:

"Tell me, dear, are you satisfied
to be foot-loose and fancy free....
you've left A Wound Time Can't Erase...."

The words were filtering back into the mind again. Oh, we'd heard the song from Stonewall on the Grand Ole Opry a hundred and one times since the early 1960s, but Floyd Cramer's version was new to us, although it has been out as long as the vocal part.

The tune lasted all of four minutes in the restaurant.

For some strange reason, we hummed it all afternoon.

'I pray for you every night'

Going back to Uncle Albert Carter's place north of Lavonia Sunday afternoon was a refreshing, yet sobering, experience.

Uncle Albert, now 85, lives alone in the rural home he shared for 13 years with Aunt Carlene Davis Carter. And he admits he spends many lonely hours each day, although three of his children live close by and the two who live away are attentive to him and his needs.

"I've got the best children in the world," he was saying.

Walking into the back of the house where we spent many happy hours with this couple and our parents tore at the heart and mental muscles.

The tree lamp is standing in the living room just as it was when Aunt Carlene left. All the furniture in the other rooms in the house is arranged the way she wanted it.

"Carlene's been dead 18 years this year," Uncle Albert was saying at the start of the conversation.

Tears flowed down our cheeks as he talked. Uncontrollable tears and a white handkerchief pulled from the hip pocked helped a little.

"Carlene was a wonderful woman, a fine wife, and mother. She loved your mother and she loved you," he continued.

There were the tears again.

In the corner sat a little white radio we had given her back in the early 1950s because she did not have an FM set, and she seemed pleased getting that.

Aunt Carlene and Mama were exceedingly close — in age, in ties, in a common bond that only sisters know.

She joined us on trips to New York City and Canada and Maine and Florida. She loved the beach and seemed to enjoy the sand and water lapping at her feet.

Aunt Carlene was one of our first teachers about country music. She told us of Hank Williams' death and remarked his going "is just like a member of the family."

She also loved wrestling, although she was aware it wasn't as legitimate as some sports. And she defended her rights to watch it on television.

She had her quota of sorrows. She spent the last 10 years of Grandma Davis' life tending to her every need as she lay in bed with what some doctors had diagnosed as cancer. But it was not cancer and Grandma lost her will to live and Aunt Carlene and Uncle Albert gave her tender, loving care.

Aunt Carlene, with Uncle Albert's help, cooked many a meal for all her 11 brothers and sisters, most of whom dropped by for Sunday dinner every week at the home place.

Uncle Albert was saying Sunday how pleased Aunt Carlene was over moving into her own home in 1952.

The two and Dad and Mama swapped visits several times a week.

Aunt Carlene never had an enemy and spoke kindly of everyone. She died in 1967 of leukemia. It was the galloping kind, but she was a brave, brave soul who endured hours of pain.

She was happiest hearing the sounds of her children and grandchildren and she placed the pictures of all in a frame beside their bed.

Uncle Albert mentioned the pictures Sunday afternoon.

"Billy, honey, Carlene's got your picture up there with the rest of the children and I see it every night when I go to bed and every morning when I get up. I pray for them each night. I pray for you every night."

That hit hard.

The tears flowed again, and we dabbed at them with a handkerchief.

There is a lesson here. People should visit more while there's still time. And time is the most precious item we have!

Family held hands and prayed

It was a touching, sobering moment.

A family of 19, including 17 related by blood and marriage, formed a prayer circle around one giant table and two small tables and Dr. Roy O. McClain, the famed Baptist minister, prayed.

He asked Divine Guidance, good health, and thanked the Maker for the food the big group was about to receive.

And then it was over, and the usual scene from a family movie of the 1940s was a real-life event in 1985 and they started passing plates.

Lunch in the largest of all rustic cottages at Pioneer Village, N.C., in this resort was a veritable feast.

Dr. McClain, who drove up early in the week with a van loaded with ears of corn, dozens of eggs, huge cantaloupes, and vegetables from his garden at Orangeburg, S.C., is presiding not over a huge First Baptist Church convention this week, but over a family gathering and he, with the help of a few younger family members, prepared food for a feast.

The table was heavily laden with bowls heaped with fresh Silver Queen corn, collards, cabbage, green beans and okra, honey-baked ham, Vidalia onions, fresh sliced tomatoes, cucumbers, bell peppers, squash casserole, dill pickles, homemade rolls and biscuits.

And dessert consisted of strawberry-pineapple mousse, chocolate chip marshmallow bars, and pound cake.

Steve Hamby of Lavonia joined us to dine with the McClain clan in Maggie Valley. The large contingent is spending the whole week in this place and a 15-mile-an-hour wind blows through the open windows of the well-kept house with a chandelier in the kitchen. A huge creek roars by on the outside and sleeping is rapid and easy.

There is a sermon and a vital lesson here.

The McClains, including the preacher, his one sister, Mrs. Ruby Johnston of Honea Path, S.C., three brothers, Paul of Montgomery, Ala., Ralph and Ward, both of Greenville, are all settled in for the week, along with their immediate family members.

Three of the McClain aunts — sisters of the late father and mother — are here, making the family circle complete.

Ward, retired at 73, was thinking out loud on the rambling front porch after lunch and pointing out that this was the second year the big family has gathered in this spot.

"That's unusual because the last time we were all together at one time was for a funeral," he said. There was a glimmer of tears in his eyes.

"Mama died at 53 and Daddy was in his 60s and the brothers and sister Ruby have kept in close contact, but we've never gotton together like the past two years," he continued.

The aunts from Honea Path and Donalds and Greenwood talked of their roots and the place in the Donalds cemetery where many of the McClain clan are buried.

This week, there is life. A group of relatives has gathered to recall and look forward and the oldest, one of the aunts, is spry at 81.

Families ought to spend more time together.

Dr. Roy O. McClain has preached many a sermon on family unity and kinship and fellowship.

Today, all week, the good man is practicing what he preaches!

An old-timer and his thoughts

The man, clad in overalls, sat in a park bench on the sidewalk of the mountain town in Northeast Georgia and summed up his feelings on the world in a few sentences.

"I think we have enough problems on our hands with the people we have here now without taking on 40,000 more with Cuban refugees," he said.

"I think Jimmy Carter done right when he told anybody would be fined and sent to prison unless they tested 'em in Cuba first," he added.

He reached into his left hip pocket for a chew of Brown's Mule tobacco.

"I may be country and mountain, but I ain't dumb," he went on. "I don't trust Castro. Never have. I think they're up to something."

He could have talked for an hour and much of what he said made as much sense as a man with a super-doctorate talking to a group of underclassmen in a University of Georgia classroom.

In fact, the world would probably be better if we employed more common sense and less textbook learning in 1980.

Since our old-time friend was born, our nation has gone through World War I, World War II, Korea, Vietnam, and only the Good Lord knows how many mini-conflicts in that time.

But he is fully aware that Cuba is scarcely 90 miles away from

Florida's shores and who knows what might be in the mind of a man named Castro?

A few years ago, our people were letting Castro speak before Congress and some considered him a hero and a leader for his country.

But discover what has happened to Cuba in the past decade and predict what might happen before 1990.

It is frightening. The whole bit.

We think 40,000 Cubans should not have been allowed here in the first place, but that's done and is history.

We agree with President Carter that the refugees should have been screened. In fact, that should have been done at the outset.

The military had a line years ago which read, "Be prepared."

Whatever happened to that?

Can media ignite World War III?

All major networks were running special bulletins last Sunday morning, almost to the point of interrupting morning worship televised live, to bring updated versions of that airplane hijacking in Beirut, Lebanon.

There it was again—all the ingredients of the years-old story, "America Held Hostage," day-by-day capsule report of American hostages held in Iran during the administration of President Jimmy Carter.

Carter caught hell from the media. The hostage situation defeated him at the ballot box. That in the midst of several matters blown out of proportion by the press.

Last Sunday's hostage situation brought President and Mrs. Reagan down from Camp David, and we didn't learn anything new from the President's conversation with the press. It was staged—much of what the Presidency has been about for more than four years now. But let that issue lie.

There is something far more important here—living and breathing Americans held hostage—this time in Beirut.

These are our people who deserve our thoughts, our prayers, but for the life of us, can't their destiny be better handled without the bright lights of TV cameras and the super-sensitive microphones of reporters and the pads and pencils of eager-beaver newsmen interested in only one item—getting the news first?

Seriously, we doubt our people would have been held hostage so long in that far-away place called Iran had it not been for that tool called the media. The Iranians orchestrated the whole affair, trying to get their point of propaganda across and into millions of American homes. They succeeded and, in the main, we lost.

Now, it happens again. Nightly, it occurs. Our enemies marched the hostages before the TV cameras and microphones Thursday night for a full-fledged press conference.

And, again, they won.

It is our contention the entire problem could be handled far better diplomatically away from the lights and the microphones and the pads and pencils.

Years ago, they should have let President Carter deliberate in his own way.

Today, they ought to let President Reagan call the shots.

Thank God, TV and the radio and the press weren't as bold and as meddlesome and as nosey, if you please, during World War II. If they had been, we might not be here today.

We end the column with a simple question: Can the news media ignite World War III by its bayonet press conference from Beirut?

There is a difference here in a public's right to know and a right to know how much, in comparison with freedom of the press.

One thing's for sure. The terrorists would lose their best weapon if America turned off its bright TV lights.

But the media in our day will never learn!

118

For love of pies and horseshoes

In September 1985, we love:
- Fresh coconut cake.
- Short sermons.
- Pretty girls who wink in the dark, but still blush in daylight.
- Home-baked pies instead of the store-bought variety served in the majority of eating places.
- A good game of Rook.
- The aroma of freshly-turned earth.
- The game of horse-shoes.
- Oldtime hymn singing from the heart without having to resort to the song book.
- The sight of the green mountains from the front porch.
- The excited voices of kids playing in the back yard.
- Hot tomato soup on a chilly night.
- Cornbread.
- Hot biscuits.
- Songs like "America the Beautiful" and "Beautiful Dreamer" and "Memories."
- Paved roads.
- Cars capable of getting decent mileage.
- Clerks who smile.
- Waitresses who smile.
- The daily adventure of retrieving mail from the rural box.
- TV game shows.
- A wholesome movie which must contain a wedding, a funeral, and a lot of life.
- And loyal readers.

Can anyone bridle a mule?

Two and a half decades ago, mules and horses, and wagons and plows were common.

On this Sunday, the question-of-the-week has to be: Does anyone out there still own a harness for a mule?

Better still, can anyone bridle a mule?

The matter came up a few days ago when Baldwin's Doyle Williams, widely-known vice-mayor of "Barstool Mountain," called the Lavonia bureau of the *Athens Daily News* and wanted a mule and a plow for a special project.

Within two hours, Doyle was back on the telephone saying he had located a mule and plow from Tommy Lee Barrett, mayor of Baldwin.

"But I can't find anyone with harness," he moaned. "It's a bad situation when you can't find a bridle and all the gear."

Gear.

That used to be an often-used word among farmers, but gear has become a one-dollar word because it went out with mules and horses and plow stocks and wagons.

Can Doyle gear up a mule?

"You dern tootin' I can," he intoned on the telephone. "Just give me a chance."

The 59-year-old former farmer, known for his unusual humor, said he checked with farmers throughout Banks and Habersham Counties and came up with zilch.

That's zero in 1986 language.

The plea for harness went out to Herbert Garrison of Homer and Bill Chandler of Commerce. They returned without a sign of a bridle or harness.

No wonder things are wild in this generation.

The situation is critical when a mule's bridle can't be found. Anywhere.

Today, it's goodbye to 'Mr. Hoyt'

Red Hill's official "greeter" is gone.

The man who waved at the world from his front porch in the rural community of Franklin County died in harness Monday morning.

Hoyt LeCroy, neighbor, friend, conversationalist first class, good man, died while watering young trees in front of his grandson's house next door to his home. He was 79.

LeCroy, known by throngs of friends as "Mr. Hoyt" or "Brother Hoyt," always called people he liked "Brother" and "Sister."

He liked a lot of folk.

The LeCroys moved to Red Hill years ago and immediately became neighbors to people for a great distance around.

Mrs. LeCroy, called "Ruby" by her husband, was in a state of shock at grandson Dean Ward's house Tuesday morning. She was remembering the many good times and how "Mr. Hoyt" helped her prepare breakfast Monday morning only hours before he died.

Mrs. LeCroy, battling a bad heart herself, was in one of the heart surgical units in Athens General Monday having a heart monitor installed by Dr. James S. Miller prior to the installation of a pacemaker.

Then she got the news of her husband's death and Dr. Miller unhooked the wires to permit Mrs. LeCroy to return home — only to start the pacemaker process all over again in a few days.

Hoyt LeCroy was a tireless individual. He wore a broad-rimmed hat to protect him from the sun, but he loved the out-of-doors and the front porch.

It was his front porch sitting that gained him southeast-wide recognition. South Carolina newsman Paul Brown featured him on "People and Places," a segment of WSPA-TV's news broadcast and "Mr. Hoyt" waved big for the camera.

He had a garden every year and was planning for the 1986 edition. He divided roasting ears and butterbeans and peas and sweet potatoes with neighbors on either side.

When he slaughtered a hog, there was sausage aplenty for the neighbors and kin.

He loved visits from neighbors and relatives, and he did his share of visiting too.

Sunday afternoon, his brothers, Tom and Otto and sister-in-law, Aldean, drove up from Carnesville and both families had a good time looking at old photographs.

121

Hoyt LeCroy used to work with the state highway department and always gave the state more hours than he was paid.

Hoyt LeCroy used to cut hair at Arthur Wood's barber shop in Carnesville and he had done his quota of front porch haircuts. He never wanted to charge a dime.

"If I can't be a friend, I ain't much of a fellow," he always said.

Family called him "Pop." He indeed was the patriarch.

Hoyt LeCroy knew much of the world from his front porch position. And he would wave anything in sight — hammer, paper sack, newspaper — at passersby.

He was a rare man in an era that needs more people of his sensitive nature and understanding of the world about him.

And this good man will be missed.

We're glad he walked among us.

Farmers' need today: friends

If there is anything farmers need in 1986, it has to be more friends.

Somehow, though, their supply of friends seems to be diminishing — all the way from Small Town, U.S.A., to the White House.

Farmers have fed the world for generations, and they have put three meals on American tables for a long, long time.

Now, they catch flak — from some men and women on the street, and from the occupant in the White House.

President Reagan's cutbacks involving the farmers touch on the Agricultural Extension Service. In the old days, they called it the Cooperative Extension Service.

These men and women have provided background information for years. They furnish tips and ideas on planting and offer the latest on insects and how to battle problems on the farm.

Suddenly, some of these funds are being cut and jobs are being abolished.

As a result, the well-known 4-H Club program is in jeopardy.

Both the 4-H Club and the FFA have been like shots of adrenaline for the farm families in bygone years.

The 4-H — hands, heart, head and health — proved to be a lifeline to better living agriculturally for millions of young people over the years.

And now, almost instantly, the Reagan administration is removing the props from some vital 4-H programs.

Part of the cuts become effective March 1 and more will take place Oct. 1.

This may be the year more farmers go under financially than at any other time since the Great Depression.

And much of it is all so foolish — and a situation supported by some powers-that-be in Washington.

Farmers have taken it on the chin for years.

They try to unite under a good, solid program like Farm Bureau, but their strength hasn't been as collective and vocal as some groups.

Lord knows, America needs the family farm and the family farm needs America.

And try to say that after going without food for only a few hours!

Ernie Pyle: A writer's writer

A newspaper had a detailed account the other day of the anniversary of the death of Ernie Pyle, probably the best war correspondent ever.

It is said that Pyle, who fought in the trenches with America's best in World War II, somehow wanted to be with the action. He was not disappointed.

The results showed in his work. We have a collection of his

war stories written from God-forsaken places that stood out like mountains in the war no one really won.

Pyle's peers said he had extraordinary guts and perception. Some even believed he felt death was not far away.

One of the last persons Ernie Pyle talked to the night before he was to be killed in combat was the late Dr. Roy O. McClain, formerly of Atlanta First Baptist Church.

We asked Dr. McClain what they talked about.

"A lot of things," he answered. "Ernie was an unusual man. He was a salty-talking individual, but everyone liked him."

Salty-talking. That's about the best way to describe a war reporter who could write about action and not a simulated nuclear incident in a place called Pennsylvania years later.

Knowing that, Ernie Pyle would have been out of place with the Washington press corps crowd today. He would tell them to jump in the lake if they started inquiring about peanuts and Watergate apartment complexes and the like.

Ernie Pyle had a feel for news. He realized what the people wanted to read, even if they had to read about his death and see his true-to-life story in "The Story of G. I. Joe."

The closer we came to knowing Ernie Pyle has been through Dr. McClain, the man who preached his funeral on that far-flung battlefield.

That was about the same time frame when Dr. McClain buried 90 American Marines before 9 o'clock one morning in World War II.

Sadly, there are no newsmen of Ernie Pyle's calibre today.

And that is American journalism's loss, quite frankly.

A different kind of vacation?

A vacation, they say, is the place to get away from it all.

Well, sometimes. Maybe.

But, for a newsman half worth his salt, he checks the papers daily to keep up with current affairs, and it was a dilly in these parts.

The Piedmont airliner which brought us here from Greenville-Spartanburg Jetport had an uneventful flight. The female flight attendants were pretty, helpful, and passed out soft drinks and toasted almonds on the leg from Charlotte to this resort town.

According to the papers, Piedmont was having a rough flight administratively. The company lost its four top people, including the chief executive officer, to Braniff Airlines because they plan to buy out the Dallas, Texas-based firm. And the June Piedmont magazine had a full page right-hand spread from the CEO telling how great things were at Piedmont and how more people will be flying this summer than ever before.

The rags were filled with the stories about a woman who kidnapped a five-day old baby and the press was playing it up for the Tar Heel people.

Up here, excessive rains are causing some damage to the tobacco group and some residents are terribly frightened of afternoon thunderstorms riddled with lightning.

North Carolina troopers were kept busy pulling motorists over who did who did not use seat belts and their law is far rougher than Georgia's. The first offense results in a warning, but the second brings a $25 fine.

Owners of the resorts are complaining of the humidity and the papers say the "unusual weather" may hurt tourism this summer. Apparently, they haven't heard of the drought encompassing Northeast Georgia and Western South Carolina.

Just like two years ago, the wire services had stories about the "greenhouse effect" that may affect the weather pattern. Funny thing though. We only heard of the "greenhouse effect" one time in 1986.

There seemed to be more grandparents with grandchildren on vacation this year — a fact that Harvey Adams of Adams' Rib Restaurant in Clarkesville brought out on early-morning TV in Toccoa.

Someone questioned the whereabouts of the parents.

"They're probably home getting a divorce," commented one wag.

Vacations can be different.

Just be sure your airline is flying. That way, you can get back more quickly.

If baseball ends, world won't

What if the baseball strike went on as scheduled — and what if the ballparks are dark for the rest of the season?

The simple truth is, such a decision would not wreck the nation's economy and could be a lesson in disguise for a country that has doted too long on athletic salaries and professional sports.

Die-hard baseball fans would stand up and violently disagree, and they are entitled to their views. Some people relax parked in front of a TV set or radio and listen to their favorite team bounce the ball around on the field.

We don't deny that.

Our argument is it is not right for a professional baseball player — or a professional athlete in any league — to command a salary of even a half-million dollars a year for a few nights' summer work.

This is particularly true in light of the fact that a college professor, who spent multi-thousands getting an education, gets a few thousand dollars a year in salary and keeps on keeping on.

It is also true when a man who turns the lathe or the woman who operates a loom spends a 40-hour week and take home just about enough money to pay the groceries and the utility bills and maybe have enough left over to splurge twice a week at the dairy bar for outside meals.

Something is wrong, and the baseball strike only points up part of the problem.

Football is just as guilty — and basketball and boxing follow closely behind.

Little wonder the youngsters, products of the TV era, are concerned when they hear the sportscasters talk about money in the millions and the kids see their own parents mortgaged to the hilt with both father and mother working.

There is a moral here — and it is that the American people ought to be the ultimate judge.

Fans should cease going to the ballparks. They should quit watching their "teams" on TV or listening on radio, and in their own way, encouraging the million-dollar-bill sports combine to roll.

The cart is pulling the horse here.

And if the lights go out in baseball, the world will not end and the cart may get a rest!

'When The Roll Is Called Up Yonder'

"When the trumpet of the Lord shall sound, and time shall be
no more,
    And the morning breaks eternal, bright and fair;
    When the saved of earth shall gather over on the other shore,
    And the roll is called up yonder, I'll be there."
                                    —First stanza of old hymn

• • •

A small church choir of Carnesville First United Methodist
sang that old hymn with gusto Wednesday night at rural Allens
Methodist Church in Red Hill.

And the choir loft probably had more feeling and amplification
than in years — and it came right before the revival sermon by Dr.
Robert Ozment, longtime pastor of Atlanta First United Methodist
Church.

Good singing of old hymns can help many a sermon and that
proved true just four nights ago.

Dennis Sullivan, member of the choir, had promised friends
they would be singing an old-time revival song and they did. The
choir members were the Rev. and Mrs. Walton McNeal, Margaret
Telford, Teresa Sears, Dennis Sullivan, Adrian Anderson, Joan
Wansley, June Sullivan, Lee Sullivan, and Martha Little. Jim
Sullivan directed and Bobbie Sullivan played the piano.

Dr. Ozment talked for 26 minutes of what he considers "the
greatest subject of all — love — the cornerstone of Christendom."

"When love comes, we can follow it with action," he said. Jesus
said, "If you love me, act like it."

"We ought to act like it," he pleaded.

And then it was over.

The final night of the three-night revival had ended, and like
most churches in 1985, it had been an abbreviated affair, but it had
been a good one, and Allens has had its quota of good revivals in
August — back in the days before the church could afford air conditioning and revival goers had to use funeral home fan to generate
a breeze.

The old hymn, "When The Roll Is Called Up Yonder," had
extra meaning only minutes after we walked into the door at home.

Jim Parten of Sandy Cross was on the telephone with the
sad news.

"Thought you'd want to know that our friend, Zeb Dean, just died," said Jim. "He was out fishing and had a heart attack. Zeb was doing what he liked best."

Within five minutes, Roger Brewer was calling on another telephone line with another message.

"Mama wanted you to know that Dad died this morning. He passed in his sleep," said the son, and there was a pause on the line. Ervin Mitchell Brewer was just 66.

And, in another 10 minutes, Dr. Roy O. McClain of Orangeburg, S.C. was on the line.

"Mike (his youngest son) and I have just gotten back from the funeral home," said the preacher. "A 25-year-old law enforcement officer from our city took his own life early today. He didn't go to our church, but he was a close friend of Mike's and he spent a lot of time on this farm as a kid. He even led the traffic at one of the funerals I preached last week."

"His dad died four years ago, and he just couldn't cope with his death," continued the minister.

And then it hit — news of three people leaving this world at a newsman's telephone within a span of 15 minutes.

The third stanza of that old hymn rang clearly through the mind:

"Let us labor for the Master from dawn til setting sun,
Let us talk of all His wondrous love and care;
Then when all of life is over, and our work on earth is done,
And the roll is called up yonder, I'll be there."

Sundays in August are good

Sundays in August are good. They also bring the memories and that isn't bad, either.

These days are perfect for family reunions and church home-comings — maybe because the weather is typically hot and people are normally in a good mood and in the right appetite for country ham, fried chicken by the tons, lemonade by the tub, homemade ice cream by the church and frosty-back pies.

Family reunions are those occasions where aunts rush up to a now-grown nephew, hug him mightily and says, "My, how you have grown. And who's the pretty lady with you?" His wife can't do anything but laugh, leaving the new hubby a little embarrassed.

Church homecomings aren't held as often as in the old days and this is bad. There are several possible valid reasons, including the fact that people don't take time to remember as much in 1985 as in 1959, and we don't stop to think of others, which is worsening by the decade too. Another factor is many of the older people who pioneered church homecomings have answered the last earthly call and aren't around anymore.

August used to be the month many churches started summer revivals, but something has happened here too. We've become so modern that revivals aren't held much in the summer anymore, and many people wouldn't go anyway. Instead, those churches which do hold meetings now hold them in the spring or fall and they generally run Sunday through Thursday nights. The morning revival service went away with Clark Gable and his "Gone with the Wind" era.

But Sundays in August are still good.

Sundays in August are good times for slicing a watermelon at mid-afternoon and sitting under the shade of an oak tree.

Sundays in August can be a good time to let the soul catch up with the body.

Lord knows, we could enjoy a lot of both!

Whatever happened to man's word?

Oldtimers used to be proud of the oneliner, "Man's word is his bond."

Maybe because it was more than just sheer talk or pure bunk.

In the old days — and we're not delving back too far — if a man told you he'd be at your house on a specific day to fix some shutters, by cracky, he'd be there. Or burst trying.

Today, big business started, and little business is following with just barely getting by, easing around the situation, or, in plain language, lying through the teeth to make a sale.

These must be symptoms of what's wrong this great country.

Over the Fourth of July, we heard much of what is right — the fireworks, the flag waving, the hundreds of speeches, the courthouse and the capitol ceremonies.

But let's take an honest look beneath some of that lacquer and veneer and admit much of today's cold-hearted business world cares not for the individual workers. Rather, they are numbers in a giant computer. Really, their main concern is the bottom line figures, profit or loss.

How, then, did we get that way?

Slowly, but surely, is the answer.

We've deteriorated from the "man's word is his bond" theory to "let's see if the price is right. I can make you a deal under the table. You stick with me, and I'll make it worth your while."

This whole problem started not with Watergate and the publicity given it, but with the Vietnam War when negativism began to invade the land.

Today, in 1988, many churches are simply dying on the vine while a few are flourishing.

Thus, the present quagmire.

Brothers don't get along with brothers anymore in many situations. And forget the sisterly love from sisters. It's as non-existent as lye soap.

Families won't sit on the same pews at church services or baseball games because of petty differences.

A noted minister summed it up in a sermon when he said Americans ought to be watching out for these signs of deterioration and noted that "a six inch tongue is the only thing that can bring down a six foot man."

Rumor, whispers, half-truths, the mania for more.

The word filtered down the line just Sunday that a friend was just getting over his second "nervous breakdown." We made a long distance telephone call, and the friend is still looking for his first breakdown, fortunately, and let's hope that doesn't come.

Certainly the Soviet leader had something in mind when he said in the early 1960s his country could take America without firing a single shot.

"We will bury you," he vowed, "by 1970."

He was a little off base. Instead, he is dead, but the intention is still the same, obviously. But what bothers us is the fact that the Soviets may be just years off base. What's that to them?

Thankful thoughts on Thanksgiving

• For another day.
• For true friends.
• For clean sheets on the bed.
• For friends who telephone and say they remember and care.
• For being aware that some people are not only two-faced but have as many as a courthouse clock, but mankind must have the wisdom to know the ring of the real and the sound of the phony.
• For antibiotics capable of destroying bugs and germs.
• For people who will get to see a Tech-Georgia game in daylight, rather than darkness as has been the case.
• For girls who say "I love you" and mean it.
• For pioneers who gave us a free country to celebrate times like today.
• For cornbread.
• For homemade pies and forget the mass-produced kind.
• For good country love songs.

- For preachers who can get their messages across inside a 20-minute span.
- For songs without profanity.
- For preachers who don't have to read sermons.
- For cool weather.
- For high school basketball.
- For college basketball.
- For professional basketball.
- For basketball.
- For pretty cheerleaders, who yell their lungs off and enjoy it.
- For good television news shows, including the likes of anchormen Tom Brokaw and Peter Jennings on the national level.
- For frosty mornings.
- For buttermilk.
- For neighbors.
- For lemonade.
- For service station attendants who check tires and windshield wipers and oil without being asked.
- For people who wave sincere greetings from their cars or say hello on the street corner.
- For a lot of people on this good day.

What's challenge chasing golf balls?

We'd like to know:
- How long frowns will remain on faces after many will fork over precious dollars at the awful hour of April 15 for you-know-what?
- How many dollars went into expensive clothing for Easter?
- Why there is so much commotion over something like the Masters at Augusta when there really isn't a lot of challenge chas-

ing a ball around an 18-hole golf course?

• What happened to America's values when dozens of men compete for thousands of dollars to become the winner of that big tournament in Augusta?

• Why some radio stations employ announcers who can't read the news wires and insist on calling Taliaferro County "Tale-e-ferro-o?"

• Whether or not oil companies really have millions of tons of gasoline stored off the American coastline?

• Whatever became of Ozzie and Harriett reruns? They were far better than some presently shown daily.

• Why TV stations don't schedule talk shows in early night when more people can watch rather than in mid-afternoon?

• Why nine of 10 patients in a doctor's office will say "just fine" when asked how they're doing?

• Why one doctor in a nearby state has maintained he aspires to say he's seen 200 patients in a day? The key word, obviously, is "see" because that's all he will have time to do.

• Why our day has more people content to work two weeks and then find an excuse to draw unemployment for the longest period possible? It seems such a waste of taxpaying money to finance a term loosely called "laziness first class."

• Whatever happened to people who gave a dollar's work for a dollar's pay?

Work day much ado about nothing

If a friend had told us a decade ago this could be a 9 a.m. to 5 p.m. era, with many breaks in a day, we would have branded it pure hogwash.

But, lo and behold here we are in an era of pushing the time clock at 9 a.m., spending three or four periods in the break rooms, and walking out the door at 5 p.m., sometimes with little work transacted during it all.

The younger generation, or part of it, would brand such goings-on work, but those of us who have seen several summers and winters resent such titles and labels describe it as a wholesale much ado about nothing.

It is, to put it mildly, totally nauseating the way many pretend to be working, even complaining about the manner in which they "really had to work today."

We're convinced only a few people really work anymore. These are the souls who put in 15–18 hours a day; often half the time in sweat and wondering why their workload is so difficult and heavy.

Of course, the reason is obvious. Those who still know about work are those who are taking up the slack from the loafers and constant gripers.

Casual observation can dictate the way to avoid work.

It works like this. Secure a job, get by as leisurely and slowly as you can, then perhaps your employers will discharge you and you can march to the nearest unemployment office for ready cash each week.

Much of our nation appears to be operating on a "why work when you can get paid for not working" plan.

And, as a result, the quality of products bought on the American market continues to deteriorate and then people have the nerve to wonder why foreign-made products hold up better than some American-built items.

Some dealers, who see shiny new cars pouring off the carriers every day, quickly tell you autos produced in Atlanta and Louisiana are often far superior to those put together in Detroit. Simply because employees returning from a drunken, carefree weekend aren't spending as much time putting cars together on a Monday.

The situation hasn't happened overnight. It's been building for years.

Maybe our generation spends too much time wondering what time it is and when the next break is scheduled and why, oh why, people have to work anyway.

Lord, where do we go from here?

The latest round of Barnum and Bailey in Atlanta — often known as the Georgia General Assembly — has its tent up and going well.

The hue and cry of some of the politicians is just like the ring announcer and the clowns who compose the mighty circus troupe.

Here is the situation in a nutshell. Lt. Gov. Zell Miller, a staunch Methodist whose devotion to church was eclipsed only by that of his saintly mother, the late Mrs. Birdie Miller of Young Harris, came out for a public vote on a lottery. That's taking the issue to the people.

The proposal found great favor in the Senate, but there were immediate thunder claps in the House after they heard from ministers, including a goodly number of Methodists, who said such a thing ought not even be talked about, much less voted upon.

The matter was shot down in a House committee quicker than a chicken hawk over a poultry yard.

Why? Why, oh, why?

It's called gutter politics—purely and simply.

You know the tomfoolery of it all?

Here are a few examples, 1989 styled:

Case number one — a Methodist church in Northeast Georgia — one that will go nameless — has put up a big marquee advertising chances are being sold on an electric kitchen device. Some of the church members became upset when a radio station told them they couldn't take the news notice because it involved a game of chance — a lottery, if you please. That is strictly against Federal Communications Commission guidelines. The church people probably went out in a huff and puff.

Case number two — three churches of a different denomination, scheduled ticket sales on homemade quilts in the last few weeks — with the lucky ticket holder getting the quilt. You're right. It's a lottery.

Case number three — and this may be the worst. Not long ago, two rural churches we know had the gall to hold cake walk sessions and bingo parties in the fellowship hall of the church. One of the churches advertised in a weekly paper and the papers didn't realize the law really prohibits them from running a game of chance.

However, all churches involved made money, and it was all one big lottery.

Now, the hypocrisy of it all.

Preachers were the main ones demonstrating — not against lottery per se, and that, too — but against taking the issue to Georgia voters to let them decide.

The question was — lottery or no lottery, and to give the voters a chance to make up their own minds.

And some legislators, with the minds of peanuts, apparently don't even want to do that.

In the long run, we're spending thousands — make that multi-thousands of dollars — to take up legislative time about something which we think ought to go to the public without any hue and cry.

If John Q. Public can pay another cent sales tax without getting to vote on it, then JQP has enough sense to vote on whether or not lottery should be voted on in Georgia.

Don't go away from reading this that Dilworth just endorsed lottery. That is not the case at all.

The point we're trying to say is that preachers — yes, even some of their church-goers — ought to clean up around their own front door on this lottery and game-of-chance issue before they start fuming and getting the nervous itch and start sounding so religious statewide.

Lord, we need you. Where do we go from here?

Uncle Charlie is unforgettable!

There's an old song that encourages others to take their sons fishing. The late Tex Ritter was one who recorded the old song "Take him fishing."

Paraphrased in 1989, a song could be entitled, "Take An Uncle To Church."

Since Dad's death of prostate cancer in 1975, his closest brother in age, Uncle Charlie Dilworth, has been exceedingly close.

Dad and Uncle Charlie were more than brothers. They were

buddies. Moreover, they were business partners in Carnesville in the early 1940s. They sold furniture, including tube-type radio sets, groceries, and watermelons.

Burnout got Dad in 1945 and he retired to the farm at Red Hill to die at 45. But he lived 32 more years because he got out in God's good world and farmed cotton and corn and hay.

Uncle Charlie stayed on. Earlier, he had established a country store in Red Hill in Franklin County and, with son, Anderson, expanded base to include shopping centers today in Royston, Lavonia, Hiawassee, and Anderson, S.C., with a fourth in the works.

This 88-year-old uncle, who turns 89 next January, is one of the most unforgettable persons we ever met.

"I believe the Bible is right when it says never let the left hand know what the right is doing," he said the other night as we carried him to the rural Trinity Methodist Church 15 miles from his home to hear his best preacher-friend, Dr. Dan Rice of Atlanta, deliver a sermon on the deterioration of home life in America.

This uncle stops at churches at random and gives big bills just because they are involved in building programs or need money. He wants it to remain anonymous.

He also finds out who is down and out with food and genuine-ly needs help and often drives to the homes to leave groceries and money. He's done that for years — all without fanfare.

This good man became close to Preacher Rice in 1952 when he served as pastor of Uncle Charlie's home church at Allens. The preacher made a pitch for funds for a building fund and Uncle Charlie did not respond that day. But he said his conscience started bothering him on Sunday night in the middle of the evening, and he got up, put on his clothes, drove to Carnesville, woke the preacher up, and deposited a rather hefty sum in his hands, but he didn't want the whole world to know at the time.

The uncle is also a right good Bible scholar. Dr. Rice made mention Sunday night to one of God's Commandments, "Honor thy father and mother that your days may be long on the earth."

"That's not a promise, but the word, *shall*, is a promise," said Uncle Charlie, who hasn't let a problem of stuttering hinder him one second.

As a young man, he didn't know his own strength. He tried out for the Georgia Tech football team in the 1920s, and the late Coach W. A. Alexander saw him cut flips and do side-bends like no other athlete on the field.

"I'll sign you up," the coach said. But a knee injury weeks later kept the uncle from playing big time.

That knee is still bothersome and it was still swollen Sunday night, but it doesn't keep him from reporting to work at Royston six days a week. He starts early — at half past 8 in the morning — and works until dark in wintertime.

He fishes a heap, but most of his fishing friends have died.

"I miss them," he said. "I shouldn't have promised my folks, I wouldn't go alone again, but I did."

The reason he made the vow came when his boat suddenly pulled his car into the waters of Lake Hartwell with Uncle Charlie behind the steering wheel.

The car became submerged and the amazing man, then 85, crawled beneath the steering wheel, rolled the left front window down, and swam to safety. He walked to a telephone for help.

Uncles and aunts can be precious souls. If you're lucky to have one or both, take them to church, fishing, or out to dinner.

In Uncle Charlie's case, almost nine decades of living have been meaningful to a grateful nephew who, like him, used to stutter so badly he couldn't give oral reports at school and college.

No wonder Dad thought so much of "Chig," as he called him. He's quite a fellow!

Sometimes it's best to remember

Dad was happy that summer day when we pulled into Shawnee, Okla., and asked how to reach the roundhouse.

"Hadn't been a railroad roundhouse here in years," said the little boy standing beside a street lamp.

It was just first dark and the day's trip of several hundred miles had taken the family across Arkansas, through most of Oklahoma and past the rivers and creeks that were beds of sand. It happens in Oklahoma when the rains don't fall.

Dad had talked for years about Shawnee, its place in the sun as a rail hub and how his Uncle Quince Adams lured Charlie Dilworth to Shawnee and how they lived and loved railroading and life in Shawnee.

"It will revive many memories just talking to some of those old-timers and seeing the place where the trains come and go," Dad had said weeks before the trip.

There was supper at the little restaurant down the street in Shawnee and a check-in at a motel not far from the downtown sector.

He wanted to see some people who would remember his Uncle Quince.

"There's just two people in town who could tell you," said the motel operator. "One is Lem Hodge and the other is Jesse Dawson. They both stay in the little two-story hotel, the oldest spot in town. Go on down. They'll be happy to talk to you."

A smile creased Dad's face because he thought he was getting somewhere.

"We're here to see Mr. Hodge and Mr. Dawson," he told the clerk in the hotel that must have been Shawnee's showplace in the early 1900s.

Then it was termite-infested, ceilings seemed to be caving, and lights hung from the top of the room.

"I'll carry you up," said the clerk.

He directed us through a narrow passageway and into a tiny elevator. It seemed an hour getting there, but it took no longer than five minutes.

"Here's Lem Hodge's room," he said, opening the door.

An old man was watching TV news on a black and white screen and he spotted his two tall visitors and motioned for us to get chairs.

"We're here, Mr. Hodge," Dad began, "to ask about Uncle Quince Adams. You remember him? He was a conductor for the Rock Island Line."

The white-haired gentleman turned a bit in his rocker, moved the volume down on the TV, and pondered over the name.

"I remember him," he said. "He was a good-looking young man and everybody liked him. But I never did know much about him. Why? You know him?"

Dad explained that Uncle Quince was just that — his uncle — and he loved Shawnee, Okla., its people, and he had long wanted to visit the place he talked about.

"Uncle Quince died many years ago in Combs, Texas," Dad said.

Mr. Hodge dropped his head, said nothing, and we looked toward the dresser in the packed room. A big railroader's watch sat on top and it was ticking.

"I was an engineer on the Rock Island for years and I think Quince was a conductor for me several times," he volunteered.

"Things aren't the same around here any more," he said. "They don't have the roundhouse, and there may be one or two trains a day. Even the bus station closes at night and the place shuts down."

There was a far-away look in his eyes. There were tears in Dad's. He told us in his lifetime how much he enjoyed the excitement of going back.

We never did get around to visiting Jesse Dawson and maybe it's just as well.

It was good dark when we walked back to the motel, around two corners and down a street, past the bus station at Shawnee and it was now closed.

Dad was thinking far ahead of us. It would've been better to remember Shawnee as it was.

Life is one shock after another

Depression, he said, hits like a tidal wave.

"I never know until it hits," he said. "Then it's like gang-busters. I think I'm going well, then it's a nosedive."

He smoked one cigarette after the other, drank deeply from a cup of black coffee, and talked quietly in the lean-to bar outside the little South Carolina town.

Paul has been a lifelong friend. He has encountered three marriages in his 32 years. All ended in divorce.

The first marriage resulted in no children. Two kids followed in the second and three in the third.

"Now what do I have to show for all that?" he asked. "Just monthly alimony and support and all that. I see the first set of kids once a month and the other three every other weekend."

"My place is like Grand Central Station the one weekend, and all are there the same time," he said. "I know it must be confusing to them. I couldn't cope with it any longer."

"That's when this mental illness hit me," he said. "I got struck with waves of depression, and the next thing I knew I was on the psychiatrist's couch."

"I've been through electric shock five times in six years. Life is just one shock after another."

"Then I've taken tranquilizers by the ton," he said. He named a half dozen kinds covering a time span of three years.

"Sometimes," he said, "I get to feeling like a guinea pig. But a guinea pig's life is better than mine most of the time."

Paul hasn't worked in months. He's on the brink of getting three doctors to declare him incompetent.

"Then I worry about what will happen to the children," he said.

Paul got up, rubbed his hands on his trousers which hadn't been cleaned in weeks, and walked out of the place.

"Don't give up on me," he said. "I'll be back. I'm hanging in there. If I can just make it through the next depression..."

Good shows go 'down the tube!'

Those of us who watch the early-evening game shows from Carolina TV stations had a bad time of it Monday night.

And all because of a politician by the name of Strom Thurmond.

Strom's no bad fellow. In fact, he is the only politician in modern times to win a major statewide office by virtue of a write-in ballot; i.e., his re-election as U.S. senator in 1968 came when he changed from Democrat to write-in Republican.

141

But Strom's persuasive, and has served in virtually every phase of South Carolina office since he was a student at Clemson.

Decades ago, they called him "Stand On Your Head Strom" because he could do just that and, at 81 today, probably would try the feat just for the press.

He did eliminate all the TV game shows on Carolina television three nights ago.

First, there was "Tic Tac Dough" hosted by Wink Martindale on Channel 13. Wink and his "x" and "o" players were axed by a 30-minute "This Is Your Life, Strom Thurmond" political ad.

At 7:30, a half hour later, Georgians watching Carolina TV knew they'd be in luck.

But, at 7:30 "Wheel of Fortune" with Pat Sajak was not to be seen on Channel 4. Instead, WYFF had the same 30-minute special on Sen. Thurmond and a glimpse of his campaign highlights.

It was a rough night so far.

Those souls who tape Channel 7 at 7:30 p.m. would normally have gotten Richard Dawson and all his kissin' cousins on "Family Feud."

Would you believe the taped replay at 8 o'clock from WSPA-TV showed the Strom Thurmond half-hour?

South Carolina's senior U.S. senator, whose name is a household word and will have absolutely no trouble getting elected again, had purchased 90 minutes of programming on adjacent TV channels in Asheville, Greenville, and Spartanburg.

Strom Thurmond was an amazing man when he won on a write-in.

Strom Thurmond was a showman when he "stood on his head" in his 50s.

And he's just as amazing in 1984 when he can pre-empt ALL the early evening games shows.

The good senator should be thankful the stations weren't in a ratings period, because it would have been a different story!

Lord, send us a good Sunday

A couple of years ago, the country ballad singer, Don Williams, had a hit record, "Lord, I Hope This Day Is Good."

One of those times we heard the song in its peak was on a cold day when a family was walking to a country cemetery to bury a loved one who had died violently.

This Sunday, past the middle of March in this year which seems speeded up and all of that, ought to be good.

It's the first Sunday after the so-called Super Tuesday, but that turned out only to be a politician's dream, which ended more in a nightmare than any other thing.

The week has been wacky in other areas too.

It's the time when one medical report said cigarette smoking is cutting short American lives. About the time ink had settled on those headlines, another story loomed in print that people who smoke cigarettes aren't likely to develop colitis.

That had to be thoroughly confusing for cigarette smokers and for people with irritable colons who probably wish they'd smoked.

The past few days produced unreal springlike weather and pretty young ladies were starting to think about taking sun baths on a warm weekday afternoon.

By weekend, some man with the handle of a meteorologist said an Arctic cold wave is lingering north of Canada and should start heading south before the end of March.

Perhaps this Sunday will be good for mind, body and soul and the country could use a long, good, quiet, Sunday—a day punctuated by a good sermon from the heart by a preacher who knows he can lose the attention of the average worshipper after 20 minutes.

Maybe there will be old time hymn singing this morning. Some churches in Northeast Georgia are starting spring revivals and the more standard churches will include "Revive Us Again" as one of the opening hymns.

Lord, make it a good day for us all.

Make it a time to reflect on the past and enjoy the present and anticipate with a degree of vitality the future!

Ah, the victuals of spring

Ah, sweet spring!

The jonquils are blooming and purpose violets are covering the sides of many mountains and cliffs.

In the early morning hours out on the farm, there is the smell of freshly turned earth. Farmers are alive again. And gardeners.

In late afternoon, there are the noises of farmers and wives with hoes and rakes making land and soil ready for the 1982 garden.

Ah, sweet spring.

That season many people love arrived just before 6 p.m. Saturday past, but, for all practical purposes, the weather-like-spring syndrome arrived days earlier and essentially skipped spring, going from winter to summer.

Some people say spring is their favorite season of all.

Others say it is their least favorite because of the elongated pollen season and the accompanying sniffles and snorts.

Nonetheless, spring is here and with it the joys and aches and pains.

Spring has changed in many respects.

In the old days, youngsters, and oldsters, too, went barefoot in the months of April, May, June, July, and August.

Hot weather saved considerably on shoe expense and, in today's business climate, that has to be a gauge.

The other day, a friend forked over $62 for a regular pair of shoes. They were not fancy. They were just plain every-day-go-to-meeting-type shoes. Fifteen years ago, a pair could have been bought for $17.50.

And it is staggering to realize that a youngster could spend a week or two in the fall picking cotton in the 1950s and not amass enough money to buy a pair of shoes in 1982.

Not many folk go barefoot anymore, however.

The "in" thing is to wear sandals and fancy slippers and dress shoes, but it is mighty costly.

Spring is a lot of things to a lot of people.

It is sitting in the shade drinking lemonade, holding the favorite girl's hand in the moonlight, or simply hearing the voices of new birds singing in some yon tree.

Ah, sweet spring!

Max teaches a little about life

A good dog, it is said, is hard to find.

A thoughtful neighbor, someone once said, is rare in 1984.

Thankfully, we have both at Red Hill.

Max, the German shepherd which hangs out at our house, was given to Mama three years ago by Dr. Roy O. McClain and his son and daughter-in-law, Mr. and Mrs. Dick McClain of Orangeburg, S.C.

Max proved he was a good dog at the start when the box carrying him tumbled open on the railroad tracks outside Lavonia and his new owner grabbed for the big dog. The animal got back into the truck and walked into the Lavonia Animal Hospital, where he made a quick friendship with Dr. Pat Hitchcock, the vet.

Max stays inside a large lot next to the house and keeps watch. He barks loudly and would bite viciously if someone invaded his territory.

Somehow, dogs have that inner nature to determine friend or foe and perhaps it would be good if human beings gained that instinct.

One of Red Hill's many good neighbors, Robert Macomson, answered his telephone the other day and offered to help when told Max was ailing.

"I'll bring my pick-up and we'll run him over to Dr. Hitchcock's," Robert said.

He was there with his truck inside five minutes and Max feebly wagged his tail at the neighbor. They are good buddies, those two, maybe because Robert feeds Max when his owners are away.

Max, weighing far more than 100 pounds, had to be lifted into the seat of the truck. He wagged his tail as he sat in the middle.

Max took note of the landscape on the way to Lavonia. He saw a few poodles and dogs of mixed breed on the 15-mile trip, but never barked.

He was too sick to bark and that's not like Max. He may be Red Hill's biggest barker when he's well and the poor animal may have been trying to tell us something when he groaned during the tornadic conditions a few hours earlier.

Dr. Hitchcock said Max had unusually high fever and ordered injections of antibiotics and steroids.

The patient was feeling better Thursday and hopefully was on his way to recovery.

Soon, if all goes well, he will be up to his old barks — greeting friend and foe and knowing the difference.

If humanity could learn the same, Russia and America and Cuba and Lebanon might be in better shape this morning.

James Miller — he watches a giant grow

Somewhere near the middle of Red Hill, between rows of cotton and bales of hay, farming was big in 1940, but the family doctor somehow found time to deliver an infant to Clifford and Sarah Dendy Miller. James Miller was born in a frame house, far removed from any grocery store aisle or the quiet corridors of a hospital.

James Miller, at 56, is one of the most amazing success stories in the grocery retail business in the southeast — and it all started when he was a youngster, no more than 12, looking at his grandfather's J. E. Dendy's Meat Market in Hartwell, when he somehow had a thought branded in his mind that he wanted to be a merchant.

A lot of things have happened along the way.

Mr. Miller, president of Quality Foods, an independent chain now covering seven stores in all parts of northeast Georgia and extending into western South Carolina, will tell anyone who asks that the secret to success has been listening to the public, keeping a basic grocery store with few fancy frills, and the policies of selling no beer or wine and no sales on Sundays.

"That has been our pledge and will continue to be our policy," said the six-foot giant as he sat in the den of his home on Lake Hartwell the other day.

But Mr. Miller doesn't spend much time in his den. Most of his hours are spent on the road, going from store to store, and helping supervise a staff of 525 employees.

He is aware that a man must remember his roots before he gets to the present. His father's first assignments were at Shoal Creek and Reed Creek in Hart County, and the grocer's son attended grade school there, finishing high school in Stephens County.

In between, they moved back to his grandfather Walter Miller's place in Red Hill, where James knew all about riding a cross-cut saw with his younger brother, David, and riding a combine, while getting all that chaff down his back, and he realized there had to be a better way to make a living.

For a while, his parents moved to the Wilhite home on the Dock Vandiver farm at Red Hill, when his dad taught school at Stephens County High School and his mother taught at Eastanollee Elementary School.

The year 1958 was the beginning of many milestones. Mr. Miller took his high school diploma in June, and all the time, knew the love of his life was Jackie Ruth Walker of Stephens County. His bride-to-be took an RN degree in Anderson, S.C. and they were married September 2, 1961 by the Rev. J. O. Anderson at Zebulon Baptist Church in Toccoa, honeymooning at Gatlinburg, Tenn., which was a long trip back in those days.

Mr. Miller credits Ed Elrod as his mentor, because he started working for Mr. Elrod at Colonial Store in 1956 at the location on Tugalo Street in Toccoa at a whopping salary of $56.00 a week.

"I'll never forget the leadership of Ed Elrod, and he remains a good man today," said Mr. Miller. Ironically, Mr. Elrod is now co-manager of Quality Foods in Toccoa.

Mr. Miller's next assignment was at the Colonial Store in Hartwell, which was opened in September, 1963, serving as head stock clerk, and then as store manager in 1965.

The Millers lived on Nancy Drive in Hartwell, where Ralph Maxwell and his wife, Barbara, live today. Mr. Maxwell is now manager of Quality Foods in Hartwell, which opened a year and a few weeks ago.

In his first jobs, James Miller will never forget his blue and white 1954 Plymouth, which could attain speeds of sixty miles an hour.

After Hartwell, he went on to Conyers, where he served from 1966 to 1972 in just about every capacity.

The Millers were in Gainesville in 1972 with Big Star on Brown's Bridge Road — an assignment that lasted until 1977.

For a brief stint, Mr. Miller worked with Colonial Store in the Toco Hills Shopping Center in Atlanta, and this is where he got his first look at a mall, because Kroger and A&P were competitors with Colonial.

He also worked at Colonial Store on Jimmy Carter Boulevard in Atlanta, and his relationship with Colonial was to encompass 23 years.

He was back to Gainesville with Big Star on Brown's Bridge Road until 1982.

The birth of Quality Foods took place unceremoniously on two fishing trips — one to Destin, Fla. and the other to Steinhatchee. One trip was paid for by CWT Farms, and among the products they peddled were Lanier Dog Foods.

"Johnny Wiley and I roomed together on the fishing trips and we started talking about a store like Quality Foods," Mr. Miller said.

The first Quality was in Commerce in 1982, when James Miller and Johnny Wiley teamed up with Verlin Reece, an ordained Baptist minister, and they opened in the old Food Giant location. At one time, Mr. Miller pointed out, Food Giant was the largest food retailer in Georgia and Big Star was second. Now both are extinct.

"We began our success by word of mouth that we had the cheapest grocery prices in town, didn't sell alcohol, didn't open on Sundays and were just plain folks," he said.

The rest is history. The second Quality store opened in 1983 in Lawrenceville and closed in January, 1996 with a volume of one hundred thousand dollars a week, but Mr. Miller says, without batting an eye, that a Georgia Department of Transportation mix-up in streets, and a labor shortage marked the end of that particular venture.

The Winder store opened in October, 1984, the Anderson, S.C. store was launched in 1986, the Sugar Hill store saw the light of day in July, 1987, the Toccoa store joined the circuit in 1989, Cornelia became a part of the chain in 1993 and the Hartwell Quality store opened in 1995 in a closed-down Winn-Dixie location; all of these in addition to the Commerce store.

"All of our stores are in locations that ultimately failed in these same spots, being large chain stores that fall by the wayside," said Mr. Miller.

He says his chain advertises in seven weekly newspapers and the daily *Anderson Independent,* and his team seeks to produce an ad featuring items that will build a complete meal for the family. "We thought that the best way to proceed is to stay the course, offer the best prices, friendly service and even carry groceries to the car — rain or shine," he continued.

Mr. Miller credits his store managers with the phenomenal success Quality enjoys today. They are David Ritcey, Commerce; Lee Best, Winder; Randall Maxwell, Anderson, S.C.; Randy McKee, Sugar Hill; Richard Burton, Toccoa; Alvin Ward, Cornelia; and Ralph Maxwell, Hartwell.

The Quality management team includes James Miller as president; Verlin Reece, vice president; Johnny Wiley as secretary-treasurer; Richard Hulsey and Ed Cook, buyers; and Frank Jones as supervisor.

The president of this super-successful chain is proud of his heritage and his parents. His dad died many years ago and his mother, 82, lives in Toccoa. His devoted wife's parents died tragically in a car-soft drink truck crash near Gainesville eight years ago.

The Millers have four children — Debbie Miller, a supervisor at the Sugar Hill location; James Miller, Jr., 26, meat department manager at Sugar Hill; Sonya Best, supervisor at the Winder store; and Stanley, 25, who has finished his first year in the US Marine Corps at Camp LeJeune, N.C.

Mr. Miller's only brother, David, is produce manager at the Cornelia store, and his two sisters, Mary Ann and Sarah Jane, live with their families in Greer, S.C.

Mr. Johnny Wiley has announced his resignation from the Quality organization, effective in late fall of 1996, but will retain ownership of J&J Foods in Gainesville, which is the largest grocery store in Hall County.

"Johnny and I have gotten along well for years, and he and I will still be good friends," Mr. Miller explained. "I'm also proud of Verlin Reece, because he is a dedicated Christian, serving as pastor and assistant pastor of churches around Commerce," he said.

James Miller points out that his family is the only Presbyterian group in the whole store chain, but the Miller clan has produced some of the finest Presbyterian ministers in the nation. A relative, Dr. Patrick Miller, was pastor of the large Druid Hills Presbyterian Church in Atlanta.

James and Jackie Miller are devoted members of Lavonia First Presbyterian Church and the Rev. Richard Scoggins, pastor, calls them "two of the most dedicated, good people I know. They are always willing to help any way they can."

James Miller relaxes by watching television, and is one of the biggest boosters of John Williamson's Carnesville-Gumlog Cable System.

The Millers enjoyed a seven-day Alaskan cruise in late summer, but returned with a bug that didn't keep them down for long.

Mr. Miller wondered out loud in this interview where that 1954 Plymouth might be rusting in 1996. The last account he had, it was sitting in some junkyard on US 123, and still carried the lettering on the windshield, "Just Married — Watch Georgia Grow."

That might have been, indeed, prophetic. Quality Foods is among the fastest-growing independent chains in the south!

Where have our heroes gone?

Country music great Bill Anderson penned a song a few years ago. It was called "Where Have All Our Heroes Gone?"

He mentioned Eisenhower and Winston Churchill and leaders in various endeavors during the 1940s, even the 1950s.

He asked, matter-of-fact-like, "And how many astronauts can you name?"

That is rather ironic since John Glenn, one of the first astronauts, spoke in Northeast Georgia at a big Chamber of Commerce banquet in Elberton Friday night.

Heroes.

They were still around, and the word was batted about in an interview with Madison County Girl's Basketball Coach Leon Fitzpatrick after his team lost by a scant two points in the last few seconds to Rockdale County.

"I felt like a little boy watching my heroes," Fitzpatrick said, referring to the shootout between Traci Waites of Rockdale and Tracy Rutledge of Madison County.

"Waites is the best guard in the country. I thought we played her super. She's better than Teresa Edwards. Teresa's good. Traci's better. (Teresa is Georgia's outstanding star, a candidate for the women's U.S. Olympic team.)

"I'm really proud of my team," said Fitzpatrick, whose girls captured the state crown back in 1981. "Especially the seniors (Caroline Collins and Donna Arndt). They meant so much to us. I thought we played our best game of the year. I really thought our players were totally prepared and played a great game. They knew what they needed to do and almost pulled it off. I feel great about this team."

Fitzpatrick should feel glad and the county is fortunate to have a man of his caliber.

He and J. B. Bearden coached many fine girl's basketball players in their competitive days when Fitzpatrick was at Danielsville and Bearden coached the Franklin County girls at Carnesville.

Coach Bearden called the Lavonia office of the *Athens Daily News* the other day to report his young girl's team had just captured the region championship in Class A basketball in south Georgia. The boys team won the region crown, marking a first for Calhoun County.

Heroes?

They're still around and you can find them in places like Danielsville and Rockdale County and Franklin County and Stephens County and Hart County.

They aren't the ones who sign $6 million per year pacts and get all the glory.

The real heroes are those Leon Fitzpatrick watched in action for four quarters the other night. They didn't get a dime for their efforts, but provided one of the best basketball games ever.

And isn't that what heroics is all about?

Jeff Walker:
meet Evander Holyfield

Even in Orange County, Calif., which boasts 11 million people, Nashville's Jeff Walker is a big man.

Mr. Walker, a native of Australia, has not missed any Billboard Music Video conferences held in this city by the sea.

Mr. Walker, who heads up Aristo Productions in Nashville, is the son of a living legend. His dad, Bill Walker, well-known music director, directs all the music for the Statler Brothers TV show on the Nashville Network, in addition to serving as music director for the Country Music Association awards program.

The young Mr. Walker, whose accent is delightful, called on our first TV-radio show in Anderson-Cornelia last Saturday night to report on the doings in Los Angeles and insisted that country music at least has its feet in the California door, but admittedly has much further to go.

The young man talked admiringly of his father during the interview, and said his dad is seen at the piano on the song of faith on the Statler show every week.

It was good visiting with Jeff Walker, who shared our table at the conference with the Rev. Jack Gillespie, United Methodist Minister of Marietta with North Georgia ties, and Greg Pitts, publisher of the *Franklin County Citizen* in Lavonia.

We laughed a lot, particularly when we told Mr. Walker it would be good to have a country act on the awards show, and he quipped, "there's no place to park the bus."

This amazing man, who has done more for country music video than any soul in America, is just as down-to-earth as his native land below us in way-down Australia.

He acknowledged on TV that his own land is as large in area as the United States, but only has a population of 16 million, most of whom reside on the coast.

Talk about room for expansion! If the corridor from Charlotte to Atlanta gets as packed as they say, it's encouraging to know there is still plenty of room a half season below us.

Jeff Walker married a young lady named Terri from Indiana and has a degree in business management. He never had the foggiest idea he would pursue the country music route, but here he is, sitting on the Country Music Association board of directors and oversees a staff of 19 capable people who supply videos for almost 200 outlets coast to coast.

The world could use some more devoted country people like Jeff Walker of Nashville and Bobby T. Tannory, who hosts his own show in Birmingham, Ala.

The last day of the trip to Los Angeles, most everyone went separate ways. Some went to Venice Beach, where all types gather including jugglers, dancers and all sorts of folk in wild-looking attire.

But, even with all that, Los Angeles, and particularly Santa Monica, seem a little more civilized today than downtown Atlanta and certainly New York City.

Our first glimpse of this place came seven years ago at the first Billboard affair, and we had pictured this place as another New York City.

But how wrong we were.

This started on a high note. Among the first passengers to get on the Continental flight was former heavyweight champion, Evander Holyfield, who had a gracious smile and signed autographs for all those who asked.

We were shocked by the fact that Mr. Holyfield is far smaller than the TV screen portrays, and it was refreshing to see that he took his seat in the tourist section instead of first class.

Here is a man who has conquered the boxing world and is worth millions, yet knows how to remain a comman man.

Sounds like Evander Holyfield and Jeff Walker went to the same type of school in different countries, and what a refreshing thought!

'Cousin Minnie' stirs the memory machine!

The Grand Ole Opry's queen of comedy, Cousin Minnie Pearl, and illnesses of veteran stars Bill Monroe and Hank Snow, revved up the memory machine the other day.

The comedienne, who was really an accomplished drama major and attended top finishing schools in the nation, lived next door to the Tennessee governor's mansion for years.

In many of her routines, Minnie talked about her home town, Grinder's Switch, Tenn., and how life was when times were not so serious and complicated.

In one of her stage appearances, while wearing that ever-present price tag on her hat, she talked about some neighbors trying to pull a stunt on women in the community by placing horse shoes in a fire before the community had a tournament. Minnie said one of the community folk handed her a horse shoe, blistering hot, which she dropped instantly.

"You don't like horse shoes?" someone asked Minnie.

"Yes," she explained, "it just don't take me long to look at a horse shoe."

Another incident in her gallery of stories involved her proclaiming she would have six women pallbearers for her funeral.

"If the men couldn't ask me out in life, they certainly won't carry me out in death," she said. That always got a huge chorus of laughter at the Opry.

Another vivid memory involved Freddie Weldon of Lavonia, who used to love to hear us tell Minnie's story of the 105-year-old man going to the funeral home to pay respects to a 96-year-old friend who had passed on.

Minnie's story went on to say that the funeral director asked the century-plus man as he reached the door, "There's not much need in your going home, is there?"

Mr. Nelson J. McBride
1725 Norton Estates Dr.
Snellville, GA 30278-2750